CHILDREN
AT RISK

CHILDREN
AT RISK

My Fight Against Child Abuse—
A Personal Story and a Public Plea
PAULA HAWKINS

ADLER&ADLER

Published by Adler & Adler, Publishers, Inc.
4550 Montgomery Avenue
Bethesda, Maryland 20814

Library of Congress Cataloging-in-Publication Data
Hawkins, Paula, 1927–
Children at risk.
1. Hawkins Paula, 1927– 2. Abused children—
United States—Biography.   3. Senators—United
States—Biography.   4. Child abuse—United
States—Prevention.   5. Children's rights—United
States.   I. Title.
HV741.H37   1986   362.7′044 [B]   86-7942

ISBN 0-91756-18-X

First Edition

Printed in the United States of America

To my mother, Mary Leoan, who believed me

There are many people I would like to thank.

My husband, Gene, and our children, Genean, Kevin and Kelley Ann, for the unwavering support they have given me. A career in public office can be a turbulent one, and their love has been a firm anchor.

My colleagues in the Senate who took the time to listen ... they helped make my legislative initiatives on children's issues realities.

William Proctor, for the organizational and editorial assistance he has provided in helping me get this book on paper.

All the individuals who took the time to contact me after my public disclosure of the sexual abuse I had suffered as a child. I was deeply touched by their heartfelt cards, letters and calls. There is a great deal of hurt in our world ... I hope this book will make a brighter tomorrow for some of our children.

CONTENTS

CHAPTER ONE

A
Personal
Story

IT WAS something I had tried so hard to forget.

Something I had discussed with no one else in the whole world, except my mother.

Something I had not even mentioned to my husband Gene—though I think he must know absolutely everything else about me.

The big secret? I had been molested as a child. I had been sexually abused when I was only five years old.

But even if I shudder to recall my personal experience, I don't want to overplay it. Compared with the terrors encountered by other victims, my difficulty was really rather minor.

Still, no matter how minor an abuse incident may seem, there are always scars. The memory of that experience had become a permanent, unspoken presence in my life—a specter I simply couldn't bring myself to share with another soul.

But a change began to come over me after I got involved in public life, and especially after I began to work for children's causes as a United States senator. My daily involvement with those who had encountered child abuse and exploitation sensitized me to the enormity of the problem. Because I had unusual access to information about the growing threat to our children, I felt a personal responsibility to make others aware of the monsters stalking the innocents in our midst. That made me more outspoken.

But still, even as I listened to story after story of child abuse and investigated innumerable cases of exploitation, I kept quiet about my own experience. I could think about it more objectively. But I didn't feel free to share it, at least not yet.

Then, I was asked to participate in the Third National Conference on Sexual Victimization of Children, sponsored by the Children's Hospital, National Medical Center, Washington, D.C. In some private, preliminary discussions with one leader in children's causes, I listened intently as she related some of the gruesome details of a pending child abuse case in California.

The effect on me was liberating. As this woman described the difficulty of getting a conviction because of attacks on the credibility of child witnesses, I had a sense of déjà vu. My abuse incident may have been relatively slight, but still, I had been here before: I was the one who was on the stand; I was the preschooler whom the adults in the courtroom were making fun of; I was the one they didn't believe.

I suppose I had been primed for that moment. For the past fifty years, I had been slowly prepared to hear what that woman was saying. And now I was poised to act.

The shameful secret I had harbored for so many decades now came to light so naturally that you might have thought that I was talking about the weather.

"It's interesting that this child abuse problem occurred in California," I said, "because that's where I lived when I was a victim of child abuse."

Stunned silence. Then: "*You* were a child abuse victim!"
"Yes, when I was only about five years old."

Finally, the coup de grace: "Oh, Paula, if you would reveal this at the conference, it would be very, very important. Would you do it?"

I had never expected such a request. But somehow, the idea didn't seem as outrageous as it might have seemed a few years before. In fact, it seemed the right thing to do.

Anyhow, I said, "Well, maybe I'll do that."

And I did do it. I was already scheduled to be on a panel at the conference. So when my turn arrived to speak, I took the microphone and disclosed that terrible personal pain of mine, the secret that only my mother and I had shared since the early 1930s.

When I was five years old, I lived with my family in a little yellow house in Long Beach, California. My father, a career man in the navy, was away from home a great deal, but I was lucky to have a very strong mother. Though petite and feminine, she was as protective of her offspring as a mother bear, and she also possessed a strong sense of responsibility about training each of us to be good citizens.

My childhood seemed idyllic. We lived in what everyone regarded as a pleasant, safe neighborhood, with lots of playmates to keep us company. Also, we were surrounded by a fine group of community-minded adults who kept a watchful eye on our activities.

There was this especially helpful couple down the block who seemed to love children so much. They made cookies for us and encouraged us to play in their home and yard. Their place even had swings on the lawn, sweets in the kitchen, and a license to run free through any room in the house.

This elderly couple's abode was considered a "safe house" where any of the kids in the neighborhood could go if their parents weren't home. We'd just wait there for our mothers to pick us up if they happened to be away on an errand.

One day, my mother was away doing some shopping, and she gave me permission to spend some time with some of the other kids down at the "safe house." It promised to be a lively day because at least five or six other children my age were there when I arrived, playing in different rooms.

The man of the house was also around that afternoon, and he looked as cheery and grandfatherly as always, with his shock of white hair and clean, neat appearance. Although he was retired, he always wore a white shirt and tie around the house when the children were there. His spectacles gave him even more of a responsible look.

At one point, when I was playing off by myself, this supposedly respectable man walked over and bundled me up in his arms. He had a piece of candy that he held out to me in one of his hands—and his other hand went immediately down into my panties.

I don't remember everything that happened in the next few moments. But I do know that he made me feel very uncomfortable. My mother had told me it wasn't acceptable for someone to touch me "in the bathing suit area." So I immediately knew something was wrong. *Very* wrong.

That half-formed, childlike sense of good and evil was probably what saved me. As soon as I could, I squirmed out of the man's arms and ran like a rabbit back to my house.

But like a lot of other kids who confront similar situations, I didn't tell my mother about the incident immediately. I recall thinking things over a bit, as children tend to do when something important—and disturbing—and perhaps a little embarrassing happens to them.

In fact, I know I was somewhat ashamed to tell my mother about what had happened. I wondered if maybe I had done something wrong.

But my mother had set up a good system of communica-

4

tion between us. She encouraged regular "talking times" when I could chat freely with her about what had happened to me during the day. Because of this warm, relaxed custom, it was relatively easy for me to sit down with her that afternoon, when our "talking time" had arrived, and let her know about what the man had done to me.

I know now that her first reaction was just right.

"You were so good to tell me about this," she said, "and we can certainly be thankful that nothing bad has happened to you. It's just unfortunate that man lives in our neighborhood. Anyhow, you must *never* go back there again—okay?"

"Okay," I replied.

And for the first time in my short life, I became afraid. Really afraid. I remember not wanting to leave my home for a few days. I was fearful of even stepping on the sidewalk—especially if I happened to be in sight of that so-called safe house. In any case, I was restricted to my yard the very same day I was molested.

The atmosphere in the neighborhood changed almost immediately. From a friendly place with open borders, the area was transformed into something resembling a high-security zone. Soon, when other parents in the neighborhood learned about the problem, *they* started asking questions—and in several cases discovered that their own youngsters had also been abused. So the parental restrictions to home and yard spread like wildfire.

Formal charges were brought against the man, and a number of the neighborhood children, including myself, began a round of interviews and hearings. But as is often the case even today, the prosecution didn't get very far. Child abuse cases are among the hardest to win because judges, juries, and other "official" grown-ups tend to believe the accused adult, not the victimized child.

Finally, the case was thrown out of court on the assumption that "the children made this whole thing up."

5

One thing that really helped this man escape prosecution was the support of his wife. She vowed that she was around the house most of the time. None of this could possibly have happened, she claimed, because her husband was too moral and upright a person. The kids *had* to be concocting the accusations, she said, and she simply couldn't understand it. After all, her husband had absolutely *lived* to make those kids happy!

Of course, I didn't understand everything that was going on in the legal hearings. But I did understand when it became clear the man would not be punished. Somehow, what the other children and I had told the court just wasn't enough. Somehow, it seemed, what he had done wasn't considered bad enough to get him punished.

The most important thing to me, though, was that my mother was comforting and supportive during the whole ordeal. I knew I was still loved and believed at home, even if somehow this molester down the street was going to go free and continue to do wrongful things to other little children.

My mother said, "We did the right thing—that's what's important."

And that gave me a sense of security and well-being that I'm sure I would never have had otherwise.

But despite the love at home, my life changed after that. I was no longer allowed a great deal of freedom. I had to be dropped off and picked up everywhere I went. Also, I had acquired a disturbing memory—a nagging thought lay tucked away in the back of my mind and made me more guarded and sometimes even fearful in the presence of strangers.

When I told this story at the Third National Conference on Sexual Victimization of Children, my long-harbored secret was picked up by newspapers and radio and television stations all over the country. The fact that I was willing to go public in identifying myself as a victim of child abuse created something of a furor—but one that seemed therapeutic for many Americans. Almost immediately, many other child abuse victims felt free to discuss and deal with their own difficult experiences. After all, if a U.S. senator had opened up, why shouldn't they?

Almost without exception, all the reactions and publicity I received were favorable. But even more important, a heightened consciousness about child abuse seemed to sweep across the nation. As article after article came out on the subject in various magazines and newspapers, I began to receive piles of letters thanking me for what I had revealed. Men and women from every walk of life said that my openness had helped them to face their own child abuse problems squarely and to begin to resolve them.

As I began to peruse the hundreds and hundreds of letters, calls, and telegrams that flooded into my office, I realized that abuse can happen anywhere, to anyone. And when it strikes you or your child, statistics and generalizations don't make any difference.

Here are a few examples of the stories that people told me:

■ "Senator, I too . . . was sexually abused as a child of four or five years of age. Only I was raped by our family friend . . . and was badly hurt. Did I become bitter? No, thanks to my godly mother."   —A FLORIDA MOTHER

■ "I [also] am a survivor of sexual child abuse. Mine continued for eight years in the confines of our house at the hands of both my father and my grandfather. . . .

"I have been greatly discriminated against . . . [because] I have been very open about my past, the damage it has done and the healing that has taken place in spite of the abuse. Child abuse is a great threat to many people, and to their illusions of themselves. . . . When we . . . speak openly about [abuse], that causes others either to confront their

7

own abuse or their desire to abuse. It brings up conflict in everyone."   —A WOMAN FROM NEW YORK

■ I saw you on "Merv Griffin" today. If only there would be a longer discussion on TV about child abuse, emotional and physical. . . . People [should] open their eyes and accept the fact that there are children being horribly abused in our great country. . . .
"As you've probably guessed by now, I have also been abused as a child by my father. The betrayal of a child's trust is the worst thing a parent can do."
                            —A MOTHER FROM CONNECTICUT

The comments of this last woman remind me of a poignant passage from J. M. Barrie's *Peter Pan*. The adversaries, Peter Pan and Captain Hook, have just met on a slippery rock out in the middle of the water, and Peter, with a knife poised, has the advantage. But when he sees that he is perched on a higher position on the rock than his foe, he decides it would not be fair to attack under those circumstances. So he gives the pirate a hand—and just as he does, Captain Hook bites him!

As Barrie writes, "Not the pain of this but its unfairness was what dazed Peter. It made him quite helpless. He could only stare, horrified. Every child is treated thus the first time he is treated unfairly. All he thinks he has a right to when he comes to you to be yours is fairness. After you have been unfair to him he will love you again, but will never afterwards be the same boy. No one ever gets over the first unfairness; no one except Peter."

That's the root of the tragedy of child abuse, especially when the abuser is a trusted relative. After all, children come into this world dependent, affectionate, and trusting. They expect the adults in their world—and especially their parents—at least to be fair with them. But child abuse

8

is *never* fair. And the youngster who experiences it, no matter how much healing or recovery takes place, can never be quite the same boy or girl again.

Unfortunately, as other letters I've received indicate, many children in our society who have suffered such a basic violation of trust never forget and often never quite recover:

■ "We want to express our thanks to you for speaking out for survivors of sexual abuse and for saying what we feel. We are a group of women who have been victims of incest as children. We are all in treatment, trying to heal the pain."　　　　—NINE WOMEN FROM NEW YORK

■ "I was a victim of incest and was not able to deal with it until after both private and group therapy. I know I could never speak of it publicly and I'm somewhat uncomfortable even writing about it. You are correct in saying that it could happen to anyone."

—A WOMAN FROM A WESTERN STATE

■ "I also was molested when I was a child. I have encountered a lot of skepticism and indifference from people as I've tried to explain what happened to me and what effect it has had on my life. . . .

"I think that every person who comes out with the truth . . . helps the rest of the population come to grips with this widespread problem. I also think that we badly need to find effective ways of dealing with both the victims and the molesters, so that we can stop this vicious cycle."

—A MAN FROM COLORADO

■ "I was a sexually abused child, and though I have . . . for the most part overcome the trauma, your courage touches and encourages me."　　—A WOMAN FROM OHIO

9

■ "I was a neglected and sometimes abused child myself. There are [memories] so painful that I have never discussed them with my husband or anyone else. Helping to raise grandchildren . . . has helped me come to terms with some aspects of my own life."

—A WOMAN FROM PENNSYLVANIA

Parents who do not accept their children's stories of abuse, and who do not take remedial action, are perpetuating the crime. Consider these letters:

■ "I am a great-grandmother, but I will never forget. It happened to me, too, when I was a child.

"My mother believed me, but my father did not. After my mother died and I had a stepmother, my father beat me and blamed me for many things I never did. How well I remember it all!

"I think you opened a can of worms. If parents would believe their children, it would save a lot of heartache."

—A WOMAN FROM FLORIDA

■ "For the sake of brevity, I will not detail my own experience. The ramifications are lifelong, among them the feelings of guilt when I was a victim!

"I attribute my feelings of low self-esteem at times to these experiences. Unlike you, my mother chose not to believe me. If a young child cannot go to her mother regarding what is going on, who can she go to?

"My experiences were about 50 years ago, but they're as vivid as if they happened yesterday. I am married to a wonderful man who is also aware of my childhood trauma, but only last year did I reveal this to my daughter. My family members really do not know how to respond."

—A MOTHER FROM WISCONSIN

Nor is the impact of child abuse limited to the young

victim. There is often a ripple effect that may reach out and touch friends, loved ones, and even caring strangers:

■ "I have been a relief society president. I don't think I can count the number of women who have told me . . . of problems of sexual molestation in their childhood and youth.

"Some women are aching to tell someone. I even had a woman once blurt out in the middle of a mothers' education lesson on communication, 'I was raped as a child of ten!' We sat there in painful silence. I realize it may have been the first time she'd ever said that to anyone."

"So many women, including myself, have these incidents in their past."   —A TEXAS WOMAN

■ "I have been ignorant of this situation for years, whether being naive or blind. But then two years ago this month, I sat on a jury regarding a stepfather accused of molesting (not rape or actual intercourse) his two step-daughters and one stepson. We six jurors knew that he was guilty. But we didn't have enough evidence to convict him.

"This experience almost resulted in a nervous breakdown. My hands were tied. I felt so confused and distraught. I can only imagine your experience and that of thousands of innocent children.

"This sexual abuse problem is an epidemic, and a most terrible and shameful burden for America. We are supposed to be humane and civilized. How can we be—when we hurt our future leaders and God's children so much?"   —A RESIDENT OF FLORIDA

■ "I am a family lawyer and, unfortunately, frequently come into contact with cases involving incest. In addition, my daughter was assaulted by a man with a knife who broke into the house where she was babysitting. The police kept asking me if it wasn't a fantasy, despite blatant physical evidence of the break-in and assault. My rage has been great." —AN ATTORNEY FROM PENNSYLVANIA

■ "I had a roommate in college who was terribly emotionally scarred because her stepfather sexually abused her for six years before her mother would believe her." —A WOMAN FROM NEW JERSEY

Unfortunately, child abuse also tends to crop up again and again, from one generation to the next in the same family:
■ "I commend you for speaking out. I know it must've been very difficult for you. I really do know because I was a victim myself as a child. As you said, 'It is an experience you never forget and affects you for the rest of your life.' I am thirty years old and just now coming to terms with it.

"As if my own experience wasn't enough, I have recently been made aware of [the] sexual abuse of my child. I have reported it, but the process is slow and wearisome. I have made known that I wish to have the man (my husband) rehabilitated rather than put in prison, but as of yet nothing has occurred." —A FLORIDA MOTHER

Clearly, many people who wrote to me were at risk as youngsters. So was I. So, perhaps, were you. And without any doubt, so are your children and the children of your loved ones. In this book, we're going to confront the dragons of child abuse, exploitation, and abduction head on—and we'll explore in depth the way those dragons can be slain, once and for all.

Some of the terrible dangers that plague youngsters in our society and often rob them of their childhood include:
■ **INCEST AND SEXUAL ABUSE.** One nine-year-old girl in Alabama ran away from home because her mother's boyfriend had been fondling and abusing her. On one

occasion, he had even had sexual intercourse with the child. In this case, the mother was quite willing to look the other way as her daughter was being exploited. The girl eventually ended up in a section of town frequented by prostitutes, and social workers got to her just before she began to participate in prostitution herself.

An estimated one out of every four girls and one out of every eleven boys will be victims of sexual abuse before the age of eighteen. Of these victims, most will be sexually abused at home by parents or other relatives. The latest figures, from the National Committee for Prevention of Child Abuse, showed 123,000 child sex abuse cases reported in 1984. But of course, many child sex abuse cases are *not* reported. Estimates for the total number of children who are sexually abused each year range as high as 500,000.

■ **ABDUCTION.** The parents of our nation are in anguish over the 1.5 million children they report as missing each year. Most missing children are runaways, but hundreds of thousands are probable abductions. Of these, the overwhelming majority are children taken by feuding parents. The remainder—and nobody knows quite how many—are the result of "stranger" abductions. Whatever the exact numbers are, all these abductions cause unimaginable heartache.

Sometimes, a child kidnapped by a parent can be in tremendous jeopardy. For example, a four-year-old girl was forcibly taken from a day-care center in Scranton, Pennsylvania, by her father. When two of the workers tried to stop the man from leaving with the child, he knocked them down and injured his daughter's head against a door as he fled.

In this case, the father already had been convicted of child abuse and a sexual offense against his daughter.

Fliers and other information were put out immediately on the father and daughter and, within a week, police officials recovered her. Had it not been for the ability of local and national agencies to respond so quickly, the risk to the child would obviously have been much greater.

■ CHILD PORNOGRAPHY AND PROSTITUTION. Many times, these offenses go hand in hand. In one case, a man was found to have some 600 pornographic pictures in his possession of young boys between the ages of ten and sixteen. He had been using these boys as prostitutes and taking pictures of them in sexual poses. He then would sell the pictures to fellow pedophiles. As a matter of fact, a "clandestine subculture" exists in the United States that is involved in recruiting and transporting our youngsters for child pornography. Such was the testimony of Dana E. Caro, deputy assistant director of the Criminal Investigative Division, FBI Headquarters, before the Senate Subcommittee on Juvenile Justice in 1982.

Over a recent four-year period, for example, U.S. Customs seized in excess of 247,000 pieces of pornography, principally in the form of letter-class mail. Between 60 and 70 percent of the seized materials contained child pornography.

Furthermore, according to nationwide estimates, perhaps up to one million boys and girls under the age of sixteen are engaged in prostitution. Father Bruce Ritter, of Covenant House in New York City, has himself counseled tens of thousands of runaways and abducted teenagers and preteens, boys as well as girls, many of whom have fallen prey to youthful prostitution.

■ OTHER PHYSICAL AND EMOTIONAL ABUSE. In one terrible case of physical abuse resulting from parental anger and frustration, a three-year-old toddler was scalded by his mother. The mother punished the child by running a tub full of scalding-hot water and then dipping the child's buttocks and legs down into it. When a social worker finally came into the case, the youngster, a black child, had already been so burned that his buttocks had turned white.

In 1984, the latest year for which such statistics are available, nearly one million children were reported as being abused in some way. And the number unreported? Heaven only knows.

■ **DRUGS.** By the fourth grade, 50 percent of youngsters nine and ten years old perceive that their peers are using drugs, according to one survey. By the twelfth grade, 94 percent perceive their peers are using drugs.

The National Institute on Drug Abuse has determined that four million Americans who either abused or were addicted to drugs in 1980 were children and adolescents of elementary or high school age. Recent studies also show that up to 50 percent and maybe more of the juveniles entering the juvenile justice system come from families that have drug and alcohol problems. Clearly, drug and alcohol abuse, either by adults or children, can be one path to juvenile sexual abuse and prostitution.

We live in a society that chuckles at the antics of preschoolers and pats toddlers approvingly. But it's also a society that neglects mercilessly the rights and welfare of those very same children. We have been guilty of great sins of omission in living up to our responsibility to protect our youth.

We blithely watch our marriages and families crumble in the interest of "finding myself" or any other excuse for selfishness. As adults, we freely pursue our own interests and satisfy whatever desires may cause us to feel "fulfilled." And our children are the ones who suffer. They are the ones who become the victims of our neglect and self-centeredness.

What has happened to our sense of compassion? To our standards of personal morality? Jesus said, "Suffer the little children to come unto me." We in effect say, "Let the little children suffer." Yet such a philosophy of life is morally bankrupt. This attitude can only undermine the self-esteem and basic character of our adults, just as it jeopardizes our children's lives.

I can speak out with particular passion on this subject because I have been involved personally with abuse. I have felt the pain in my own emotions and psyche.

But even as the memory of the pain lingers, I've become convinced there is a way out. There are practical steps we can take to minimize the dangers and rescue many of those children who are at risk.

Before we discuss concrete programs, however, I want to let you know a little more about the aftermath of my own disturbing childhood experience—and how this led to my involvement in children's legislation.

CHAPTER TWO

The Road to Legislation

WHAT effect does child abuse have on the young victim in later life?

It depends. It depends on what kind of abuse was involved, on the intensity and frequency of the abuse, on the child's own special personality, and on a host of other particular facts and factors.

According to a July 1985 Senate report, the manifestations may begin with emotional and learning disorders, poor school performance—and over time, may lead to suicidal and delinquent behavior. One study cited by the report said that "many incest victims, particularly those still searching for some way to make sense of their experiences, show psychological disturbance 20 years after the assaults."

Some children who have been physically abused go on to abuse their own offspring. Those who have been victims of incest may find it extremely difficult to form enduring, loving relationships as adults. Children who have been abducted and later rescued may live in the presence of unremitting and unnamed fears and anxieties. And, of course, there are thousands who are abducted and never see their homes again.

We'll be considering these and other issues further in the following chapters. But for now, I want to continue speaking personally. What was the effect of the abuse that I suffered as a child?

I was lucky. The molestation in my life was comparatively minor and short-lived. Also, I had supportive parents—and especially a warm, compassionate mother—to see me through any emotional trauma.

There were even some effects that made me wiser and more discerning as I matured. For one thing, I became more wary of strangers. Certainly, I wouldn't recommend that any young child be subjected to threats, fears, or abuse just to learn how to protect herself. But because I had learned firsthand about exploitation, the warnings from my mother acquired additional meaning.

I know that my abuse incident confirmed my mother's decision to be strict with me and my siblings in our interactions with strangers. I was taught that if she told me to stay in one spot and wait for her, I was to *stay*. That meant not wandering off even one inch to the left or right.

She had also instructed me that it was wrong to be touched in the bathing suit area. And if I *was* touched there, I was to report to her immediately. Of course, that's exactly what I did. I'm convinced now that if I had not been taught these things, something much worse could have happened to me.

By all rights, I was so well prepared that I should have avoided being abused at all. That's what's so alarming about my experience. I shudder to think what might have happened if my mother had not been as savvy as she was.

So, if I was the obedient child before the abuse incident, I was *extra* obedient afterward. I never gave my mother any trouble whatsoever. If she said "no," I'd just say "okay," without a bit of argument.

Still, this is not in any way to say she was some sort of martinet. We were always great friends. In fact, after I got a little older, many people thought we were sisters because we related like siblings and looked much alike.

Also, we continued our "talking times" until I finally left home for college. We talked about absolutely *everything*. I can remember that as an adolescent, when I got a crush on a boy, I could tell her about it. I didn't feel I had to run off and tell some girlfriend—my mother was the best listener for me.

When my father came home from one of his navy trips, however, tension could develop over techniques of child rearing. He was a much looser, devil-may-care type. When I went off somewhere with him, he tended to give me much more freedom.

For example, when we lived in Georgia, my father was a very popular figure in the community and was often asked to chaperon at dances at nearby Georgia Tech. The school would invite big-name band leaders like Tommy Dorsey and Benny Goodman to play for the dances. Even though I was quite young, maybe twelve or thirteen years old, my father would talk my mother into letting me go with him.

"She'll just sit in the bleachers and listen," he would say. "She'll remember the experience of listening to these big bands. It'll be good for her."

"All right, but she *cannot* dance!" my mother would say. "She's too young. If any of those boys ask her to dance, she can't."

He would always agree. But inevitably, one of the Georgia Tech freshmen would walk over and ask me to dance. And my father would wink and let me accept.

"Just don't tell your mother!" he would say. "If you do, we'll both be in big trouble."

Of course, my mother would eventually find out, and

she would get a little upset. She thought that he wanted to show me areas of life that were beyond my youthful grasp. It's true, as my father argued, that I was quite mature for my years. But my mother sensed, rightly I believe, that such activities and experiences could easily wait until I was a little older and better able to handle myself.

There's no question that this strict upbringing shaped my own philosophies of family relations and child rearing. I kept very close tabs on our three children until they were old enough to care for themselves. But my husband and I didn't try to remove all the fun from their lives—quite the opposite.

We did everything possible to encourage them to have their friends over. We were fortunate to be able to provide plenty of recreational facilities. We bought a pool table, invested in a piano and lessons, even went to the expense of building a swimming pool. Our home in central Florida became the neighborhood center for kids to play. But like my mother before me, I laid down plenty of rules for them to follow.

For example, it's almost impossible to find hills to play on in Florida. So we built a hill in our backyard for the kids to use. Unfortunately, they began to pull each other down the slope on pieces of cardboard, and all the grass began to come out. That called for a rule: "No sliding down on cardboard."

Also, to keep watch on what was going on with the youngsters out in the back, we installed glass doors looking out over the deep lot in back of our house. That way, I could see everything that was going on. My son began to call me "the hawk."

Occasionally, some child would protest about the restrictions we placed on play. But such griping didn't bother me—and it certainly didn't seem to bother other parents.

One of our neighbors told me, "Oh, you have the greatest yard around here!"

"We enjoy your boys," I said. "But one of them told me the other day that there are too many rules in our yard."

"Well, he doesn't have to go to your place if he doesn't like it. As for me, I appreciate that you have rules for him to keep."

"And he *does* keep the rules when he's with us," I said.

We have always felt that if we made our home as much fun for the youngsters as possible, they would be more likely to *stay* home. Consequently, they would expose themselves at a young age to fewer dangerous, threatening, or questionable situations. In short, they would be less vulnerable to negative outside influences until they were ready to cope with them. Also, the more they were around us, the more opportunities there would be to establish lines of family communication.

My husband quickly picked up on my own sensitivities about the vulnerability of youngsters. He had encountered practically no supervision as a child because his mother, widowed early in her marriage, had been forced to work. The result? The kids in his family could do pretty much what they wanted.

Sometimes, Gene would skip school for two days in a row. Like most of the truants in those days, he'd head straight for the local pool hall. To be sure, he became an accomplished pool player. But if he hadn't recognized early on that this activity wasn't going to get him anywhere in life, he'd probably still be shooting pool instead of pursuing a rewarding career as an engineer.

Because of these early experiences, Gene was really down on pool as a pastime. When he would lay down the law for our son, Kevin, you could almost hear the baritone of "Professor" Harold Hill from *The Music Man* railing against pool in "River City."

There is a fine line, of course, between being *too* restrictive with children and not restrictive enough. If you come down too hard on them, they may rebel. Or sometimes even worse, they may be too self-conscious to share any experiences they may have with abuse or molestation outside the home.

However, if you keep track of their activities so that they become convinced you're really concerned about them, you'll position yourself as a "good ear." And you'll be more likely to hear about your children's problems and concerns.

It was a relief to me to learn our younger daughter Kelley regarded me as a confidante on at least one abuse-related occasion. She came to me about a problem she and some of her classmates had experienced on a school trip.

This out-of-town jaunt was something that the youngsters in her school had looked forward to a great deal. But when she returned from the trip, she said that an accompanying adult had tried to have sex with some of the young girls.

She asked me, "Should I be one of the people who confirms what happened?"

"Do you have any firsthand knowledge?" I replied.

She said that the man had put his hand "where he wasn't supposed to" on one of her classmates, and the girl had slapped him. After our discussion, the incident was eventually reported to the school authorities—and the man was prohibited from further involvement with the youngsters.

Of course, I was quite relieved that this molester had been removed from the local scene. But I was even happier that my daughter had come directly to me with the matter.

There's no question in my mind that my early childhood upbringing and experience—including the experience with abuse—have had a profound influence on my own approach to motherhood and family life. I always have been alert to danger. I have tended to listen for the sound that isn't quite right. I feel I am far more cautious than most parents or grandparents because I'm highly attuned to possible danger signals when one of my loved ones seems at risk.

This watchfulness and wariness also influence how I deal with other people's children. When they visit my home or, for some other reason, I have responsibility for them, I treat them with the same protective care that I give to my own.

In short, I'm somewhat of an extremist when it comes to protecting families and upholding family values. My feelings and convictions run so deep that early on, it was easy for me to become militant in family matters, whether in my own home or on a broader, political stage.

My first foray into community and family-oriented political action focused on a sewer system—specifically, the sewers for the city of Maitland in central Florida.

After we won that battle, I became more deeply involved in politics—including election as Republican national committeewoman and as Florida State Public Service commissioner. Finally, in 1980, I won some tough primary battles and became the Republican nominee for the U.S. Senate.

Predictably, some of the major issues that emerged in the Senate campaign centered on my specialty, the family. But I'm afraid I didn't always respond in quite the way my opponents *or* supporters anticipated.

I was known to many people as a conservative who was a strong supporter of *traditional* family life. So there was an assumption among some people that I'd probably say such things as, "The wife has to stay at home," or "Children should only be cared for by their parents." In fact, many people concluded that I would probably be against any form of child-care or day-care centers.

But during a statewide television debate, I set the record straight when I was asked what I thought about such facilities.

"I've always had a deep conviction that the best child care is provided on-site, where people work," I replied. "Why should a mother or father take a child across town for day care? Suppose the child gets sick with a temperature? Then you have to leave work, run over, pick the child up and take him home. That takes far too long, both for the parent and the employer."

This answer surprised my own political team and that of my opponent as well. Perhaps they had expected me to come out with some predictable antifeminist statement. But I've found that most issues, including family-related ones, are more complicated than that.

As a matter of fact, as I pointed out during that Senate campaign, I'd had firsthand experience with day-care centers when I was a young mother back in the early 1950s. Working as a secretary in a big furniture company in Atlanta, I became distressed that I couldn't spend more time with our first daughter, Genean.

At the time, I *had* to work, just as many mothers today must hold down a job. So I investigated the child-care situation thoroughly in Atlanta and finally selected a center that I felt would be right for Genean.

I inquired about the credentials of the owner, how many people worked there, and how much experience they had. I also asked how much money the employees made. In my opinion, it's important that day-care workers not just be helpers but that they have professional positions that command a decent salary.

Also, I often walked into the day-care center unannounced to pick up Genean. I never let them bring her out to me in the car. The reason? I wanted to see what was happening inside the center when they weren't expecting a parent to show up.

In the back of my mind, I was always influenced by the example of my mother, who was deeply concerned about where and under what circumstances children should be left with other people. After all, she had learned the hard way—and so had I! My own experience of being molested was a constant presence with me. Consciously or subconsciously, it provided a note of warning as I tried to make the best possible arrangement for my own daughter.

The place I finally settled upon was much less convenient than several other likely locations. Although the closest center was run by a director with very good references, I just didn't like her very much. For one thing, her establishment didn't seem all that clean. There was something about her manner with children that bothered me. My intuitive reaction to people, especially where child care is involved, has always been important to me. I think most mothers are well-advised to follow their instincts in determining who should care for their own children.

Ironically, another avenue I had investigated before I settled on a day-care center for Genean was my own company. My reasoning was logical. There were many women working at this place, and almost everyone had a child. I knew many of them had the same problems with day care that I faced.

So I approached my boss and asked, "Why don't we have a corner where we can care for the children here?"

His response? "We're in the furniture business—not in the children business."

Of course, that was 1951, and on-site child care was an idea somewhat ahead of its time. But the refusal still rankles—especially when I think that if my boss had agreed, I could have spent several extra hours each day with my daughter.

The place I finally picked wasn't very near my work: I had to drop her off at 8 A.M. and then go and pick her up at 4:30 P.M. In the process, I lost valuable play hours with her as I was commuting back and forth.

During the Senate campaign, my practical experience with

such issues as day-care centers began to emerge, and I suspect this made it much easier for many female voters to identify with me. After all, I had been through many of the problems that they were facing. I was sensitive to the need for resolving them, not just ignoring them.

In any case, when the votes were finally counted in November of 1980, I found myself headed for the Senate. In just a few short weeks, I would be inducted as the second woman then holding a Senate seat. To be sure, I expected that some interesting struggles and confrontations awaited me in the halls of the nation's capital. What I did not realize was that, through a series of unforeseen circumstances, I would emerge as a leading advocate of actions and legislation centering on children and the family.

CHAPTER THREE

Missing Children

O BVIOUSLY, I have always been family-oriented. So I was delighted that responsibility in this area was more or less thrust upon me as I prepared to take my seat as a member of the new Republican majority in the Senate. It had been more than twenty years—during President Eisenhower's first term—since Republicans had wielded control of the Senate.

That meant that even new senators were going to have to assume major responsibilities as heads of committees and subcommittees. I became a member of the Senate Committee on Labor and Human Resources, of which Senator Orrin Hatch was the new chairman. He had worked to help me in my own senatorial campaign, and we had become quite close. I felt comfortable serving under him.

Soon I assumed the chairmanship of the Subcommittee on Investigations and General Oversight. As the title of the committee indicates, I had an open-ended mandate. I could look into what was being done to promote and implement legislation on anything to do with labor or "human resources."

That suited me just fine because I had always been a "human resources" person, ever since my initial involvement in politics and public life. In fact, I had seen myself as such a person since my adolescence and the beginning of my marriage. "Human resources," as far as I was concerned, meant anything to do with the needs of people and especially of families.

But still, I wasn't sure what sort of legislation I would focus on—at least not until an article came across my desk about a missing child in New York City. I'd never heard of the case at the time, but it was swiftly gaining nationwide attention. The incident concerned the abduction of Etan Patz, a six-year-old boy who disappeared when he was walking to his school bus in Manhattan.

I immediately called the FBI to see what they had done about the case. At the time, I still had the naive notion that such kidnappings were part of their duties. Although the FBI's charter says that it is supposed to look for kidnapped children, I learned in my first hearing on the subject that it preferred not to have anything to do with most missing youngsters. It thought these cases resulted mainly from parental squabbling or the acts of delinquent children. In sum, it didn't want to get involved.

But that didn't satisfy me. Child abduction was too close to child abuse for me to dismiss it so lightly. So, I fixed my sights on the problem of missing children.

That meant holding a series of hearings to investigate why certain children had disappeared, what exactly had happened to them, and what could be done about it. The incident that I focused on in those early days of investigation was the case of Etan Patz.

At one hearing conducted by my committee—at which Senator Ted Kennedy, our chief counsel Jay Howell, and various other staff members were present—Julie Patz,

Etan's mother, told her story eloquently. Here is an edited version of the tragedy from her testimony:

At 7:50 A.M on the morning of May 25, 1979, I said good-bye to my six-and-a-half-year-old son, Etan. It was the first time he was to walk the one-and-a-half blocks to the school bus by himself.

The school bus was clearly visible from in front of our home, and there were other children and parents waiting there. I discussed procedures one last time with my son, Etan, and I watched him walk the first half-block with only one block left to go. Then, I turned and went back into my home. That was the last time I saw my son.

At 3:30 that afternoon, at the time my son usually returned from school with another parent, he had not done so. Ten minutes later, I phoned the parent who usually walked him home from the bus stop, only to find that he had not arrived on the bus. This parent checked with her daughter, a classmate of my son's, and was informed that he had not gone on the school bus that morning. Also, he had not been in school the entire day. The school had not called me to notify me that my child had not arrived.

At ten minutes to 4:00 that afternoon, I telephoned the local precinct to report my son's disappearance. After lengthy questioning about my relationship with my husband and our relatives, and repeated reassurances by me that we were not involved in a custody fight or other family dispute, they agreed to send a squad car to our home.

Two officers arrived one hour later. They checked with my son's school and confirmed that he had been absent that day. They then contacted the precinct house for additional help.

It was the start of the Memorial Day weekend, and many people had already left the city, while many more were prepared to do the same. Time would be an important factor. Our son had already been missing ten hours when approximately three hundred police officers began a rooftop-to-basement search of the buildings in our immediate neighborhood. A temporary police headquarters was set up in our home.

That was the end of life as we had known it. Almost two-and-one-half years have passed since that day, and we still have no clue as to our son's whereabouts. The result: Unbelievable disruption of our lives—disruptions over which we have had little or no control. This turmoil persists, with no end in sight.

At one point, Mrs. Patz said, she and her husband found themselves being regarded as suspects by the police. Their personal and professional lives were subject to constant strain as they worried about Etan and what was happening to him.

Subsequently, there was a report that a New York taxi driver had given a ride to a man accompanied by a boy fitting Etan's description. The man was said to have been urging the youngster to go with him to an undetermined location. Also, there were later press reports that a youngster fitting Etan's description had been sighted in Israel.

The Patz family, of course, confronted a very particular and individual set of circumstances, which is unlikely to be repeated precisely. But the fact remains that many, many youngsters are abducted in one way or another every year in this country. And countless more suffer other forms of abuse.

Moreover, when the Patz tragedy came to my attention, there was no mechanism to get the federal government involved immediately in missing children's cases. There was no imperative placed on the FBI or Justice Department. As a result, no central communications and investigation center existed to coordinate a nationwide search. And this lack of overall control could be a decisive deficiency in those essential early efforts to find a missing youngster.

So, my major mission was apparent to me. Granted, I could have headed in any number of useful directions with my committee. But we have a southern expression: "You can get your dog into too many fights." You can get involved in so many areas that you lose your effectiveness. This was a danger that constantly faced me as chairman of

the Subcommittee on Investigations and General Oversight. So I decided to home in on the missing child issue
until it was resolved in some way.

One test that I used to justify this decision was to ask
myself the question: "If today were my last day in the
Senate, what would I do?"

My answer: I would try to pass legislation on missing
children.

This was a natural route for me to take. I have always
been responsive to children's needs. I had taught Sunday
school until the time I was elected to the Senate, and, in
one way or another, had always been around young children. Working with youngsters was in our family tradi-
tion: My mother had been an outstanding teacher, and I
was always impressed when grown men would come up to
her later in life and say, "You had such a profound effect
on me as a young person."

As I began to get more involved in politics in Florida,
the problems of children were always paramount. We had
a drug problem in the state back in the mid-fifties, and by
the 1960s it had gotten completely out of hand. Unfortunately, much of the drug abuse involved children. Also, I
had served as chairman of a Chamber of Commerce committee on drug abuse for one year in the 1960s. That got
me even more deeply involved in the subject.

Part of my early concern had focused on the problem of
what we called in Florida "drifter-children." If you drove
regularly up and down the highways, you could see these
youngsters, many of them preteens, thumbing rides and
looking so shabby and vulnerable. They obviously had a
mother or father somewhere—I knew the kids hadn't been
issued by the government! But the big questions remained:
Where were the parents, and what was to be done with the
children?

This problem of drifter-children intensified during the

late 1960s and early 1970s. The social problems got worse and worse as many of the youngsters moved into crime, drug abuse, and prostitution.

In a number of ways, I was prepared for a Senate crusade to do something worthwhile to protect the nation's vulnerable children.

For the next year or so, as I plunged into the missing children issue, I learned how important it is for freshman senators to do their homework. First of all, I took a careful look at what legislative activity had gone on before—and I learned that Congressman (later Senator) Paul Simon of Illinois had introduced a bill about missing children in the House of Representatives. But it had languished there without a great deal of support.

Usually, there's such pride of authorship in legislation in Congress that it's almost impossible to take over somebody else's bill and make it yours. But Simon had no such misplaced sense of pride. He was mainly interested in helping missing children. He knew the Patz family and had tried to help them find Etan. So, he was more than willing to get behind my effort to push a bill through the Senate.

When I started out, I knew next to nothing about Senate procedures or protocol. As a result, I made plenty of mistakes as I tried to get some momentum built up behind the missing children's bill.

For example, I knew it would be very helpful to get other senators to cosponsor the legislation with me. But what I didn't know was that it was customary for senators to send an aide or page around with the bill. Instead, I walked it around myself, buttonholing as many senators as I could find and asking, "Would you like to sign this? Do you want to cosponsor this with me?"

When I went over to the office of Senator Howard Metzenbaum of Ohio to make my pitch, I got an extensive lecture-and-lesson about Senate proprieties and protocol. He began with a friendly reprimand: "Senator, you haven't been in Congress too long, and I have. So let me tell you something. Number one, you don't wait outside in my waiting room. A senator comes straight in to another senator's office. Number two, you don't walk these bills around. You send a page or you send an intern."

"But it's important . . ." I began.

And he interrupted: "If it's important, we'll pass it."

As unorthodox as my methods may have been, however, they did seem to be working with this particular bill. I ended up with more than eighty cosponsors—the overwhelming majority of the Senate.

But as well as we were doing on the Senate side, it wasn't quite good enough. Unbeknownst to me, a considerable wave of opposition had been building up in the House, primarily because of pressure from the Justice Department and the FBI. Those agencies just didn't want to get into the problem of missing children. They were afraid they would get mired down in family fights, such as when one divorced or separated spouse steals a child from an estranged mate.

In any case, my bill—in amendment form—ended up in a House-Senate joint conference where the final legislation was to be hammered out. But I was unprepared for the sequence of events that occurred.

The room was very crowded. There were so many lobbyists and legislators that they seemed to be sticking out the windows. I think there's an element of strategy in the way rooms are chosen for these conferences. There seems to be a tendency to pick the smallest room in an effort to smother any opposition.

To make a long story short, I lost. The joint conference failed to reach an agreement before Congress adjourned. That meant if we wanted to pass the Missing Children Bill, we'd have to try again the next session.

It was all so discouraging, especially since I felt it was a battle that could have been won. With more than eighty senators cosponsoring the bill, it should have passed the joint conference in some form.

At that time, I just wasn't sure how best to marshal my forces for a winning effort. But I learned. And one of my greatest allies was John Walsh, a parent whose own child had been abducted, and who was as committed to the missing child legislation as I was. Without his untiring efforts, I honestly question whether the bill would ever have become law. To understand why he felt so deeply, it's helpful to listen firsthand to his story in this edited testimony from one of our subcommittee hearings:

> On July 27, 1981, at approximately 12:30 P.M., our only beloved son, Adam John Walsh, was abducted from the Hollywood Mall, in Hollywood, Florida. He was six-and-a-half years old, and a superior student in private school. Adam, a member of his T-ball team, was a very disciplined little boy with great respect for authority figures.
>
> Adam and his mother, Reve, had been shopping in the Hollywood Mall. He was in the toy department, with his mother approximately three aisles away. In a matter of ten minutes, he vanished. What proceeded has been called the largest manhunt in south Florida history.
>
> After Adam was paged in [the store], the Hollywood police were notified and immediately proceeded to search for Adam. Hundreds of volunteers belonging to the Citizen Crime Watch, as well as thousands of individuals, joined the search. The Florida Fish and Game Commission, as well as the Florida Park Rangers, searched the area within a fifty-mile radius. Helicopters searched day and night; private planes joined the search during the daytime. Divers in boats joined the search in canals and quarries.
>
> An initial reward of $5,000 was offered, and that was rapidly raised to $100,000 by pledges from concerned business associates and strangers. The vice president of Delta Airlines called from Atlanta and offered to send three hundred people down to join in the search. Both Eastern Airlines and Delta Airlines helped by delivering posters [about] Adam's disappearance to airports in cities all over the United States.
>
> By one final count, over one million posters were printed

and delivered throughout the United States. A private postal delivery service hand-delivered thirty thousand posters each day to different areas throughout [Florida's] Dade and Broward Counties.

After approximately three days, the organized search was abandoned, and it was determined that Adam apparently had been kidnapped. The Federal Bureau of Investigation was contacted, but they did not enter the case. [They stated they needed] evidence of Adam's crossing the state line with his abductors, or a demand for ransom.

A massive media campaign was then mounted to inform the public in the Florida area about the disappearance of Adam. The three major television stations in south Florida carried news of Adam's disappearance on every newscast at 12 noon, 6 P.M, and 11 P.M

On August 1, we attempted to alert the entire state with the full cooperation of Orlando Mayor Willard D. Frederick, Jr. We flew by private plane to Orlando and held a press conference for all the major television, radio, and newspaper people.

Disney World briefed their three hundred security guards and twenty detectives. Busch Gardens, Circus World, and other facilities cooperated in the search. A representative of the family also flew to Atlanta and appeared on Ted Turner's Cable News Network, which broadcast news of Adam's disappearance.

During this time, the FBI was constantly updated but [the agency] never officially entered the case. A family friend received a call from Attorney General William French Smith's office and was assured that the administration would see that everything in their power was done. But again, the FBI never officially became involved.

Because of the difficulty and oftentimes the apparent lack of cooperation between different police agencies, members of my [John Walsh's] office staff spent three days and nights contacting by phone every police and sheriff's department throughout the state of Florida. We also personally mailed five flyers to each office. Hollywood police continued their round-the-clock efforts as their fine detective bureau followed every possible lead.

Over sixty psychics from around the country—many recommended by certain police agencies, as well as psychics who had received notoriety working on the Atlanta child murders and in Los Angeles on the freeway killer murders—joined the case. Many other police agencies throughout Florida cooperated, though some others politely ignored the problem.

After approximately four days of constant coverage in the media, eyewitnesses finally began to come forth. One boy apparently thought he had seen Adam leaving the store, followed by a burly man in his late twenties or early thirties. He said the man was a white male with dark hair. The man had reportedly run from the Hollywood store and jumped into a blue van, which almost hit the boy and his grandmother as it screeched away.

Then, there was a report from a female security guard in the store. She felt she might have asked two sets of arguing boys to leave the store. Possibly, Adam, who was watching them argue over an Atari video game, may have followed her instructions and left reluctantly with the other boys.

After close investigation, the detectives determined that the security guard's version was the most likely, because of Adam's great respect for authority figures. In other words, he probably followed the orders of the security guard and left the store with the other boys. The consensus of opinion is that he would never have left the store on his own.

Adam had traveled extensively with me and my wife and had never become lost or wandered away from us on any occasion. He lived across from a park, but was not allowed to go into the park by himself, nor to ride his bicycle in the street. He never had a strange babysitter; he was always looked after by my mother, who lives with us, or by my younger brother.

On August 10, my wife and I flew to New York for an appearance on the "Good Morning America" show. Early in the morning, as my wife slept, I was notified in our hotel room that a young boy's head had been found in a canal in Vero Beach, Florida. I was told that the remains might possibly be those of Adam. But there was a need to obtain his dental records and deliver them to Vero Beach.

[Despite this news] we went ahead with the "Good Morning America" show. Host David Hartman asked me if we really wanted to go on with the show. But I informed him that even if the remains were those of Adam, I felt we should tell our story because of all the other missing children.

So we appeared on "Good Morning America" at 8 A.M to plead for Adam's safe return—and for all [our listeners] to recognize the problem of missing children. Upon our return to the hotel at 11 A.M, we were informed that the remains that were found in the Vero Beach canal were definitely those of our beloved son Adam.

The unending nightmare had now become a reality as we flew back to Florida.

I might have lost the first battle in the fight for national missing children's legislation, but I wasn't about to lose the war. Not with the tragic experience of John Walsh constantly before my eyes.

CHAPTER FOUR

Defeat into Victory

J OHN WALSH became a highly motivated lobbyist for the missing children legislation after our first defeat in 1981. That's rather unusual, given what he and his wife, Reve, had gone through.

It's understandable for victims, and relatives of victims, of child abuse and abduction to turn the other way. Many want to escape, to flee the unspeakable anguish they have had to confront.

But not John Walsh. He looked directly into the face of horror—the unprovoked, senseless slaughter of an innocent child—and was still able to move ahead as a children's advocate.

But it wasn't easy. As he told our Senate subcommittee, even as we worked to pass the legislation.

> For us personally the nightmare continues. Two possible, but not probable, suspects in Adam's case are now in custody.
>   The first suspect recently raped and bludgeoned a six-year-old boy and left him unconscious near railroad tracks in a remote area of Florida. The boy subsequently died in the

hospital, never regaining consciousness. In the effects of the suspect was found a diary. It logged and evaluated in his own perverse terms the homosexual rape, assault, and possible murder of twenty-five victims, young boys ranging in age of ten years and younger. The acts of violence were carried out throughout two states in the last two years.

A second suspect, in custody in an eastern state, a twice-convicted child molester on parole, had newspaper articles concerning Adam's tragedy pasted throughout his room. This suspect described approximately forty-five incidents throughout four states during a three-year period. Subsequently, in a mini-warehouse, the gruesome articles of his twenty-year career were discovered.

Among the effects found were six sets of small boy's clothing; pornographic literature dealing with sadism; detailed diaries; correspondence with another child molester; and grisly tools of his trade: whips, chains, paddles and sticks, as well as cassette tapes.

As I listened to the tapes, I saw tears in the eyes of six streetwise, supposedly hardened homicide detectives, listening to the screams, cries, and pleadings of those young voices. Hoping against hope not to hear the sounds of my own son's voice, I became physically ill. I will never be able to forget those cries. . . ."

Yes, it's understandable to turn away permanently once you've looked such horror in the eye. But John Walsh is stronger than that. He knows that the statistics indicate that thousands of our children are abducted each year by strangers, many of whom are perverts and sadists.

He also knows the frustration and futility that most parents face as they search for their lost children. He says, "We can never forget the looks on their faces. They still search for their children, determined that no matter what the cost, emotionally or financially, they will find them. In most cases, [it's] a hopeless cause."

But still, Walsh has refused to look away.

In fact, he says that he and his wife Reve "have determined that although we would never be able to find any answers to Adam's death, he would not die in vain. We thought that the best way to deal with our grief was to do something for the rest of the missing children in the United States."

So with the donations they received from people sympathetic to Adam's death, they set up the Adam Walsh Child Resource Center, which now has offices in Orlando and Fort Lauderdale, Florida; Cleveland, Ohio; Orange County, California; and Rochester, New York. The purpose of the Walsh Center is to provide information and assistance to parents of missing children through a telephone hotline. Also, the Walshes continue to travel around the country, telling the story of the problem of missing children "to a nation that is obviously unaware that this problem exists."

A major way in which John Walsh contributed to the cause of missing children was to join forces with me and the Senate Subcommittee on Investigations and General Oversight as we made our second attempt to pass the Missing Children Bill. John soon became an expert witness on many aspects of exploited and abused children. He was particularly adept at discussing the subject from the parents' point of view.

The purpose of our legislation was the same as it had always been—to use existing federal resources to help the parents of missing children get information about their youngsters disseminated nationally. Without such information, police in a different city could find a missing child—or worse, a child's body—and not know who he was.

In the past, there had been an experimental system for putting facts about missing children into the National Crime Information Center (NCIC), which is an automated data base maintained by the Federal Bureau of Investigation. The NCIC provides information to federal, state, and local law enforcement agencies throughout the United States, Canada, Puerto Rico, and the U.S. Virgin Islands. Among other things, the data bank stores information on wanted persons and stolen property, as well as other criminal statistics. The system operates twenty-four hours a day and can supply facts immediately through any NCIC terminal to authorized criminal justice agencies.

The problem before 1982 was that parents lacked a clear-cut right to have information about their missing children put directly on the NCIC computer. Parents had to work mainly through local law enforcement agencies, and many of those agencies were not aware of the NCIC or how it operated with regard to missing youngsters. Also, some of them just didn't want to bother with parents' requests.

In addition to greater parental access to the NCIC computer network, we wanted a specific requirement that the federal government would help identify deceased persons who had not been identified within a reasonable period of time. (We thought fifteen days after the discovery of a body was reasonable.) So, if a child disappeared in Texas, his identifying characteristics could be cross-referenced with a body that might be found in Nebraska.

We wanted to get the federal government more involved from the outset in finding missing children. To make the point explicit, we provided that the law be cited as the Missing Children Act.

Our bill was designed to authorize the U.S. attorney general to acquire and exchange information that would help him assist federal, state, and local officials in the location of missing children, and some adults as well. Under the bill, federal agencies could collect and use information to assist in the identification of any dead person or in the location of any missing person who was:

• in the company of another person under circumstances indicating that his physical safety was in danger;

- missing under circumstances indicating the disappearance was not voluntary; or
- "unemancipated" (i.e., a minor, or one under the protection of a parent or guardian).

But the FBI was fighting us. One of their strongest supporters, Assistant Attorney General Robert A. McConnell, wrote a strong criticism of the bill to Senator Strom Thurmond of South Carolina, the chairman of the Committee on the Judiciary.

McConnell stated that the Department of Justice had previously opposed enactment of the bill because it was "concerned that direct parental access to the National Crime Information Center would be counterproductive and raise false expectations in the minds of parents of missing children."

He added, "It continues to be our position that the investigation of missing children complaints is primarily the responsibility of local law enforcement agencies."

This was the sort of high-level opposition we were dealing with in 1982 when we walked into our second House-Senate joint conference on the measure. But this time I was better prepared.

There were still plenty of objections to getting the federal agencies involved in looking for children. One suggestion from our opponents—who were beginning to realize that they might not defeat the bill—was a compromise slanted in their favor. They proposed that there should be a forty-eight-hour period before missing children would be listed with the FBI. That way, there would at least be a delay before the Justice Department had to get involved.

At that point, I turned to Strom Thurmond and asked, "Strom, how many kids do you have?"

"I've got four," he said.

"How old are they?"

He told me their ages.

Then I said, "What if one of those children disappeared?

43

Then suppose you go to the police station, and they say they'll list the youngster as missing after they've checked into the matter. Then, you call the FBI, and they say they don't have any jurisdiction for forty-eight hours."

I continued with my hypothetical example, much of which paralleled the Adam Walsh case. In that situation, the parents—despite the help they received from many sources—got knocked back and forth like Ping-Pong balls between various agencies.

Before I could finish my story, Thurmond interrupted: "Just a minute, just a minute! While all this is going on, who's looking for the baby?"

I'll never forget that response. Who's looking for the baby? That was a classic.

"Nobody," I replied. "Nobody but the mother and father."

"We're passing this bill!" Strom declared.

That was one of the most dramatic moments of the entire conference for me because I knew that the momentum was shifting in our direction. Despite all the attempts at amending and watering down, support seemed to be building to *mandate* the FBI to get into a missing child case immediately.

Finally, the time arrived for the vote.

Senator Thurmond, as chairman, was sitting at the end of the table, and I was right next to him. Next to me was Senator Hatch and a row of the other senators. The House members were on the other side of the table, with our main opponents almost directly across from me.

It was tense for all of us. I had been working on this—it had really been my life—for nearly two years.

As the roll was called, the votes for and against were fairly even. It was obviously going to be close.

We had worked our "Senate side of the street" quite well, and most senators were solidly behind the measure. Also, I had encouraged mothers' groups to contact all the House members and bombard them with phone calls and telegrams. It's true that some congressmen were troubled by these tactics. They told me later they didn't mind the bill; they just objected to our style.

But I replied, "We didn't have time to be gentle."

Now we were at the moment of truth. The ayes and nays kept coming, one after the other. It was dead even, right until the very end.

Then we came to Congressman Jim Sensenbrenner of Wisconsin, a Republican who had originally indicated he might not cast a vote. But this time, he did vote. He voted "aye" and with that, the bill passed! By one vote.

For the supporters of the measure, this was a moment etched permanently in our memories. Orrin Hatch turned and embraced me. I saw out of the corner of my eye that John Walsh, who also was attending the conference, was standing there by himself, crying and crying. So I turned around and grabbed him and hugged him. Soon those tears that were streaming down his face had mingled with my own.

That may have been the most moving moment in my life. I knew how essential the legislation would be for the nation's families. But it was also an important victory for me personally, and I certainly knew how important it was for John Walsh. The meaning and remembrance of Adam's life and death had come to hinge for him on this one moment.

Of course, the bill didn't become law until President Reagan signed it. That was a deeply moving event, too, with John and Reve Walsh there to bear witness, along with all the other supporters of the measure.

The story of Adam Walsh, the fight for the measure, and the president's signing of the bill into law was finally told to the entire nation through the television presentation "Adam."

The battle has continued on the legislative front, with considerable success. The Missing Children's Assistance

Act, which I cosponsored with Senator Arlen Specter of Pennsylvania, was passed in 1984. Among other things, this law established the National Center for Missing and Exploited Children, provided grants to communities to promote child protection, and established a toll-free hotline for information on missing children.

With all the new legislation, it was clear almost from the outset that we had taken a major step forward in winning this battle. Parents could now, without any time delay, move to enter their children on the "Missing Persons File" of the NCIC. Of course, the FBI still has the right to check with the local law enforcement authorities, to make sure the case is known to them as a legitimate one.

But still, the outlook is very encouraging. Parents have considerably more power to get full descriptions of their missing youngsters disseminated to law enforcement agencies throughout the nation.

For example, Ricky, a fifteen-year-old mentally retarded youngster took a train to an East Coast city with some of his friends. But some time after they arrived in the city, his friends thoughtlessly gave him some money and told him to return home.

Because of his mental handicap, he became lost, and soon his worried father was calling the local police department to report the child missing. The police just told the parent not to worry—and didn't enter the father's report into the NCIC computer system.

For months, Ricky's distraught father spent every spare moment looking for his son, handing out flyers and conducting personal searches for miles around the area where Ricky had last been seen. Finally, the National Center for Missing and Exploited Children learned about the case and encouraged the local police department to enter the boy's name with the NCIC. Also, Ricky's picture was aired on national and local news media.

Only slightly more than a month later, the National

Center's hotline received a report that a boy who looked like Ricky was in a children's shelter—and *had* been there for almost eight months!

It seems that Ricky had been found by police in that East Coast city, but because he was unable to identify himself, the boy had been placed in a shelter. In this case, unfortunately, the national mechanisms for finding a child were not employed as soon as they might have been. But when they were finally used, the youngster was returned home safely.

Despite these successes, I soon learned that the war to protect our children must be waged doggedly on a far-ranging front—with the constant danger of political combat fatigue.

The personal stresses came from several quarters. Friends would approach me with their own problems about abuse—incidents they, like I, had never told before to a soul.

For example, one acquaintance of mine had been abused by a family member. But her mother had insisted, "Don't ever tell, because we would all be humiliated."

So she kept the terrifying and debasing incidents bottled up inside herself for years and years. Then, after the publicity from my own work with missing children and child abuse—and especially after my disclosure about my own experience—she felt free to talk.

She was just one of many who sought me out for personal advice. After a series of speeches and other public appearances, I increasingly found myself becoming a kind of on-the-spot counselor, both for friends and also for perfect strangers.

Women would come up to me at a forum and say, "Oh, let me tell you what happened to me when I was a child." And I would listen and sympathize—but not without considerable draining of my own psychological and spiritual reserves.

I found that no matter how much support I received from my immediate family, there were times I felt I was reaching the end of my rope in dealing with the onerous burden of child exploitation. It was difficult enough, listening to the graphic testimony of people like John Walsh and Julie Patz, who had lost their children to twisted child abductors. But the feelings that I experienced hearing their stories intensified even more when I visited hospitals that cared for the many young children who were abused.

I would cry inside, and sometimes quite openly, when I saw those youngsters burned with cigarettes or viciously beaten. They were so vulnerable. Yet they were prime prey for parents and others whose perverted minds drove them to inflict torture on little ones who should have been receiving only love.

Finally, a major reason for the constant pressure I felt was that the war to protect children was never over. Big battles continued to occur in the glare of public scrutiny and heavy press coverage. Sometimes, the most hard-fought—and stressful—engagements occurred on the arcane battlegrounds of government bureaucracy and funding.

Despite the strains of this ongoing political war, the effort seemed more than worth it when I received in 1984 the designation from the Juvenile Justice Coalition as "the Children's Senator." The award was a statue called "The Runaway," based on a Norman Rockwell sketch. It depicts a clown wiping a tear away from a thin little child. Every time I look at that figure, I remember the *real* missing children—and I feel like wiping away a tear or two of my own.

The Juvenile Justice Coalition is composed of professionals around the country in the fields of detention, crime prevention, and education. They are dedicated, grass-roots workers who have devoted their working lives to the cause of children.

To them, I might be "the Children's Senator." But I know I still have a long way to go to reach the level of service to children that these workers have already achieved. And as I investigated even more extensively the heartrending area of child exploitation and abuse, I became increasingly aware of how much work there remained to be done.

What's the current status of the missing children dilemma? To put it bluntly, if your child is missing from home for any reason, the risk that he or she will be criminally or sexually exploited rises significantly.

Jay Howell, now director of the National Center for Missing and Exploited Children, reports that 85 percent of children who were victims of criminal or sexual exploitation were missing from home at the time they were abused. Also, the center's investigations show that "up to 11 percent of the children who have voluntarily left home, end up as victims of criminal or sexual exploitation."

In short, the more of our children who are missing, the more there are who face the risk of abuse. But exactly how many *are* missing? There is some controversy on this subject, largely because of the deficiencies that exist in our governmental reporting systems.

The U.S. Department of Health and Human Services has indicated that 1.5 to 1.8 million children are reported missing each year. But this number may include such youngsters as:

• the teenager who stays out all night and causes worried parents to report him or her to the authorities;

• a teenager who runs away three or four times a year and is counted as one missing child for each incident;

• the youngster who is taken home by an estranged parent without the other parent's permission—and then reported to law enforcement officials as missing.

Somewhere between 50 and 90 percent of the 1.5 mil-

49

lion or so missing youngsters each year are runaways, and a large number return within a few days. Also, as I've indicated, one child may be counted repeatedly if he or she runs away more than once in a year. But remember: if a child is missing *for any reason*, the risk that he or she will be abused in some way greatly increases.

In addition, we have to deal with the large number of missing youngsters who are *not* runaways. Hundreds of thousands of youngsters are missing each year because they've been taken away, most often against their will. In perhaps 90 percent or more of these cases, the children have been snatched by estranged parents in custody disputes.

Parental abduction, in itself, may be considerable cause for worry. As we've seen, most sexual child abuse takes place at home. So, a child who is abducted by a parent may very well be placed at risk of being abused by that parent. In any case, it should be up to court authorities and not estranged parents to determine where that child will live.

Even excluding parental custody disputes and runaways from the statistics on missing children, we are still left with a significant number of "stranger abductions." There is some controversy over how many children are taken each year by someone they don't know. Recent estimates have varied from as low as 4,000 to as high as 50,000.

Now, I realize that this is a very broad range. By any standards, there's a big difference between 4,000 children and 50,000. But again, keep in mind the difficulties that we have in gathering figures.

For one thing, it's not always clear, especially when a child is older, whether he or she has been abducted or is a runaway. Also, different governmental and private agencies have different definitions about what constitutes a "missing" child. Some agencies will report a child as missing when a parent or legal guardian so requests. Others may wait from several hours to several days before they will record the youngster as a missing person. Then, whether the child is finally classified as "abducted" or not will depend on the evidence that law enforcement officials gather and the judgments they come to, based on such evidence.

As for me, I'm inclined to agree with Jay Howell. He says he believes somewhere between 4,000 and 20,000 children are abducted each year by strangers.

But when you think about it, does it really matter whether the number is 4,000, 20,000, or 50,000?

Rather than quibble over how many are abducted by strangers or estranged parents—or how many are missing for some other reason—let's take steps to *reduce* the number missing! Let's protect them from exploitation! No abstract statistics should distract us from the plight of even one innocent child who is in danger of any kind of exploitation. And the kinds of danger a missing youngster may fall into are sometimes too horrendous for words.

CHAPTER FIVE

Sexual Exploitation

WHAT is child abuse?

A wide variety of practices may constitute abuse by almost any definition—including physical beating and the infliction of many forms of psychological pain. But usually, when we think about abuse, sexual exploitation comes to mind. This insidious form of victimization, which seems to be increasing and even running rampant in our society, includes everything from minor molestation to incest. In addition, some children fall prey to pornography and prostitution.

Sexual abuse of children is a problem that has always been with us. But as a society, we've either been ignorant of the problem, or we've chosen to avert our eyes. After all, sexual molestation is an embarrassing, messy stain on our social fabric.

During the relaxed, relatively prim-and-proper American culture of the 1920s through 1950s, many adults were aware that children were being sexually molested. But often the matter involved Uncle Harry, Aunt Sally, or

53

some other family relative. So, to avoid scandal and embarrassment, it was rarely talked about. In fact, quite often the sexual abuse was simply denied. In a nice, well-bred American family, how can one possibly admit the existence of anything so sordid?

But ignoring or denying the perversion didn't make it go away. Not in modern-day America, not in the Middle Ages, and not even in ancient Rome. Roman aristocrats and emperors, like Tiberius and Caligula, were reported to take babies off their mother's breasts and bring them into court so that they could be initiated in sexual practices from toddlerhood on up. Young boys or young girls—the sex didn't matter. All that was important was immediate gratification of adult emotional and physical cravings.

Unfortunately, these callous abuses are not limited to ancient times. And most of the sexual molestation of children occurs at home. Sex abuse and incest are so closely linked that it's impossible to discuss one without at least mentioning the other.

Some letters I have received highlight the personal scope of this tragedy in our society. In some cases, these letters may begin to point the way to the light at the end of the tunnel, the ways in which this terrible problem may eventually be overcome. But in every instance they reveal a degree of heartache that should inspire our sympathy and cause us to take steps to protect our children.

For example, consider the plight of a nine-year-old girl who was betrayed by a trusted relative:

■ "I lived with my own terrible secret for 28 years, keeping it even from my husband.

"I was nine years old and was abused by a favorite uncle. But when I told my mother about [the abuse], she didn't believe me. She said that if it did happen, I must have done something to make him want to do it.

"I was somehow able to make myself forget or push it

54

out of my conscious memory [the exact nature of] what he did. But I will never forget the guilt I have felt all these years because of her words to me. It's true that it affects you for a lifetime.

"Recently, my secret finally came out. I was seeing a . . . psychologist, trying to deal with my father's death, and I was finally able to admit what had happened. I am so thankful that I have had such an . . . understanding counselor."

Now, imagine a homeless young boy, desperately seeking the solace and security of a strong father figure. And try to understand the shock he experiences when he discovers his adoptive father is, instead, a cruel man obsessed with his own gratification:

■ "Having been abused myself, I am very much aware of the emotional trauma that an exploited child goes through. [As a young boy], I felt shame, disgust, anger, frustration, helplessness and guilt. And I still feel [these emotions].

"I was adopted by . . . a [homosexual] sadist. I was the victim of numerous harsh beatings, which were unprovoked and unjustified.

"As a 66-year-old male, I've experienced a lot of emotional problems. Even today, when I see or hear of an abused child, it literally tears me apart because I know what that child faces. In my opinion, any person who is abused or molested as a child never completely gets over it. Still, I'm glad that the news media is at long last drawing attention to this disgusting practice."

But perhaps the most devastating kind of sexual abuse—and betrayal—is that which comes from a natural parent:

■ "So often, we are made to feel guilty, alone and frightened. I am a 27-year-old woman who was physically abused as a child. I was around ten when it started, and the episodes continued for several years. The abuser was my father.

"The terrors can follow you through adulthood. Young children need to be helped because it's difficult for many of them to know the difference between 'right touching' and 'wrong touching.' Also, for a small child, the word 'no' is sometimes useless against threats of lost love, punishment and retaliation by an older, stronger person. . . . The result may well become a . . . rape of the innocent.

"Yet there are many thousands of women, and men as well, who would be willing to join together and fight this problem if they just knew what to do. I only need to know what I can do in my area. And I'd also like to know what can be done for those of us who have borne the guilty shame for so many years.

"Our children are our future, and they need to be protected. . . ."

If things are relatively safe and secure for a child at home, that's no reason to become complacent. The letters I've received often cry out with the anguish of parents who thought all was well, until they discovered that a place like a trusted day-care center had become a living hell for their infant or toddler:

■ "We are the parents of a small child, who, between the ages of 14 months and 19 months, was sexually abused at a day care center in our area. The . . . abuser was a family member of the day care provider.

"We fully agree with programs that teach children to protect themselves and to tell their parents about abuse. But one group of children and parents is being missed. These are the pre-verbal children, the young toddlers and infants who can't communicate well. These children can't be taught yet to protect themselves, nor can they tell their parents or anyone else, should something happen to them.

"[With] all the emphasis and publicity on the sexual abuse of children, more abusers seem to be turning to younger toddlers and infants—because these youngsters simply can't protect themselves. The abusers can get away with it!

"More emphasis needs to be given to what parents of pre-verbal children should be alert to—what signals or behavior may be signs of abuse. Before this happened to our daughter, we did not know what behavior to watch for. Parents need to be warned that no child is too young to be sexually or physically abused."

So often, children seem to become totally helpless when they are victimized by molestation. No matter where they turn, they can't seem to find help—or even anyone who will believe them. And the anger and emotional damage can reach far beyond childhood:

■ "I am thirty-four years old. From the ages 5 to 13, I was sexually molested by a man that my mother had married. (I say 'a man' that she married, because I refuse to consider him a stepfather.) The same man sexually molested my brother. I did not find this out until a year ago.

"Although it took me a long time, I finally told my story when I was 13 years old. I had always been threatened by this man. He said, 'If you tell, I will say it was all your fault.' So I had never told before because I felt that my mother would side with him.

"After I did tell, my mother took me to a female doctor to have a vaginal examination—because the 'man' had had sexual intercourse with me. After the examination, I dressed and returned to the doctor's office. But the first thing the doctor asked was, 'Are you sure that you haven't been with a little boy?'

"To this day, I will not forget those words. She was saying, 'I do not believe you—you are just making this up.' So I can just imagine how other children feel when a judge calls them liars.

"This [experience] has caused a lot of grief in my life. I have not been able to have a lasting relationship.... The psychologist [whom] I went to said that it is because I don't trust my feelings with anyone. It's really hard to go through life not having anyone to be close to.

"Recently, I went to a lawyer to see if I could sue this man. She said that the man would have to have some property or money before I could sue. She also said the judge would probably tell both of us to get professional help. Well, I've had a year of professional help at my own expense, and I feel this is enough.

"I also went to the police, and they said that a person can only be charged for this kind of crime up to two years after it happens. [In my case], it has been too long since it happened for them to do anything about it.

"I would like to have a bill passed in my state to allow an adult survivor [of abuse] to have the molester prosecuted. To make an adjustment to normal life, the victim of abuse may have to go through analysis, and the cost of this service is not cheap. [As you know], a person can be tried *anytime* after he has *killed* another person—and I think the crime of abuse is much like murder. Why should a person who has destroyed *parts* of a person's life go free after a couple of years?"

Stories like these are just the tip of the iceberg. In a typical year, an estimated 100,000 to 500,000 American young-sters will be sexually molested—though most of these incidents will never be reported to any authority. In fact, according to the Family Violence Research Program at the University of New Hampshire, nearly one out of five American women and one out of ten American men have been sexually molested as children. The Program estimates that between two million and five million American women have been victims of incest alone.

The statistics on sexual abuse can never be completely accurate because many incidents are never reported. Still, other experts back up the far-ranging scope of the problem reflected in the New Hampshire findings.

For instance, Dr. Vincent J. Fontana, the medical director of the New York Foundling Hospital, says that his studies have shown that at least one out of every five girls and one out of every nine boys is abused sexually by an adult during childhood. Also, 80 percent of the time the abuser is an adult whom the child knows—and usually a family member. Dr. Fontana noted that fathers are much more likely to abuse their children sexually than are mothers.

Other studies have delineated the nature of sex abuse even more precisely. One Cornell University investigation of cases in the Bronx in New York City found "a significant relationship between the victim's age and the place where the abuse occurred."

In general, the study revealed that preschoolers were victimized *outside* their homes—and the offenders tended to be under age forty. In contrast, teenagers were more often abused at home by a father or stepfather. The ages of the offenders in the cases of the teenagers tended to be from forty-one to sixty-five.

The Cornell researchers also found that 66 percent of the victims were age twelve or younger, and 19.3 percent were under age five. A couple of particularly disturbing findings: Almost 30 percent of the youngsters were abused for as long as a year; and 21 percent were sexually abused from ages one to three years.

What are the effects of this sex abuse on the victims?

The Cornell study discovered that the youngsters old enough to attend school did poorly in their studies, with those who were the most seriously abused doing the worst.

Our own Senate subcommittee investigations have also revealed emotional and learning disorders as well as delinquent and even suicidal behavior. Furthermore, the effects may linger long after the abuse has ceased. In a 1984 article in the *Journal of Social Issues*, the author found that "many incest victims, particularly those still searching for some way to make sense out of their experiences, show psychological disturbance twenty years after the assaults."

It is clear from what various Americans have revealed to me that sexual abuse at home can indeed affect a child for life:

■ "I too had instances of 'fondling.' Thank God, nothing further happened. I was afraid to say anything.

"I'm now 44 years old, but I can still vividly recall those horrid moments. I know that it's affected my life."

—A RESIDENT OF FLORIDA

■ "I speak from experience regarding the long-range, devastating effects of child abuse. I'm almost 42 years old and have just recently been learning to come to grips with the effects of the abuse I suffered as a child.

"While I was growing up in an abusive environment, nobody was interested in the subject of child abuse. Therefore, it 'didn't occur.' . . . Children are victimized for a lifetime, but the guilty parties—the abusers—are allowed to go free and usually commit more abuse."

—A WOMAN FROM IDAHO

The aftershocks may be expressed in alcoholism, feelings of low self-esteem, and various emotional problems—as the experience of this woman clearly demonstrates:

■ "I have never written to a Senator before, but I recently read an article about your personal testimony at a Conference on Sexual Victimization of Children . . . . You give me hope that I will someday be able to talk about my father's sexual abuse of me without being shamed and feeling somehow responsible.

"Until I stopped drinking four years ago, I had forgotten his abuse and the rest of my childhood. I am now 34 years old, and for 13 of those years, I was drinking and drunk—and I did not even know why. I thought there was something wrong and bad within me. Now, I am in therapy and I am learning that there is something wrong—and it is not me. I am worth . . . loving.

"I just want to say that when I read about someone who has gained the strength and love to share that terrible secret and feel stronger, I feel stronger about myself. That is the key—education and talking to each other. It is the secrets that kill us." —A WOMAN FROM ALASKA

Why is sexual abuse of children so prevalent? In part, the problem stems from the fact that many disturbed adults are walking our streets and inhabiting our homes, just waiting for the opportunity to prey upon innocent youngsters. But there's also another reason—the fact that in our Western societies, we often make it relatively easy and may actually encourage the activity of pedophiles.

On one level, sex researchers have joined the popular media to suggest that it may be all right in some cases to participate in incest. Typical of this trend is an article in *Time* (April 14, 1980) entitled "Attacking the Last Taboo: Researchers Are Lobbying Against the Ban on Incest." In that report, one leading sex researcher is quoted as saying, "A childhood sexual experience, such as being the partner of a relative or of an older person, need not necessarily affect the child adversely."

Other experts are quoted variously to the effect that: "It is time to admit that incest need not be a perversion or a symptom of mental illness. . . . Incest between children and adults can sometimes be beneficial. . . . Children have the right to express themselves sexually, even with members of their own family."

Behind such thinking is the assumption—absurd on its face—that young children are actually capable of making an independent judgment about their own sexual activity when confronted with pressure from adults.

The Dutch government is even moving toward codifying this assumption in its laws. They have proposed to lower the age of sexual consent from sixteen to twelve years of age. In other words, it would be legal for adults to have sex with minors as young as twelve so long as the youngster had not been coerced or seduced with gifts or promises.

But I wonder, how can a child *not* be coerced if an adult is given free rein to exert moral and emotional pressures?

In the face of such societal pressures, what can be done to reduce sex abuse and incest in the home?

Researchers at the University of Utah have concluded that the answer may be a more intensive paternal role for fathers in bringing up their infant daughters. The researchers found that fathers who actively hold, feed, and diaper their female offspring in the first three years of life are less likely to abuse those girls sexually later.

Other studies have shown that sexual abuse of children in families may be linked to the father's lack of sexual fulfillment, his lack of satisfying social interactions, and the prevalence of drug abuse.

But even if inroads are made into reducing child sexual abuse in the home, it's likely that pedophiles will continue to look for vulnerable prey. For example, one child molester from New York told Senate investigators he had abused twenty-two young girls, sometimes by seducing them when he was babysitting. He said that he had actually paid one father one hundred dollars to "rent" his daughter!

"I used all the normal techniques used by pedophiles," this offender, who was imprisoned in California, said blandly. "I bribed my victims. I pleaded with them. But I also showed them affection and attention they thought they were not getting anywhere else. . . . I used these kinds of tricks on children all the time. Their desire to be loved, their trust of adults, their normal sexual playfulness and their inquisitive minds made them perfect victims."

This molester, who admitted that he himself had been abused as a twelve-year-old, said that one of his techniques was to show prospective victims pornography involving other children. Then, he'd say, "It's okay! See, these other children do it."

The frightening thing is that sexual abuse can occur almost anywhere, at any time, under a variety of circumstances. So, it may be hard to predict just where a molester will commit his next offense. Consider this range of recent cases:

• In October 1985, three eight-year-old girls were sexually assaulted by a male intruder in their school bathroom in the South Bronx.

• A Long Island high-school student reportedly hired a classmate to assassinate her father. She said her parent had been forcing her into an incestuous relationship with him.

• A United Methodist minister was found guilty of sexually abusing five children in a Bronx day-care center run by his church. He was convicted on nineteen counts of rape, sodomy, and sexual abuse, involving four boys and a girl, aged three to four.

• A three-year-old Denver girl was approached by a stranger while she was playing outside her Denver home. She got into the man's car—and was found three days later standing almost nude in sewage at the bottom of a park outhouse in the Rocky Mountains. Doctors discovered upon examining her that she was suffering from, among other things, sexual abuse. An alleged attacker was soon captured.

• Another three-year-old, a youngster from San Francisco, was abducted from her parents' car while they were inside a store. Her abductors kept her in a van for nearly a year, forcing her to engage with an eleven-year-old youngster in rape, sodomy, and other abuses. When her abductors were caught and the case came to trial, color snapshots and home movies that the abusers had taken were placed into evidence. The graphic display drove some of the spectators from the courtroom. The two abusers were finally found guilty of forty felony charges.

• A teacher's aide at a day-care center in the Bronx, who was accused of sexually abusing children under his care, was convicted of twenty-five assaults on five youngsters.

Clearly, we are confronting a veritable plague of crimes against our children. What's the solution?

Unfortunately, there may not be any ultimate "solution" as such. There are indications that it's impossible to cure many pedophiles of their sexual problems. Consequently, there are probably always going to be perverts roaming the streets, waiting to prey upon unsuspecting children.

The only real answer to this situation, it seems to me, is *protection.* Parents must learn to identify the dangers and then help their children avoid risk-filled situations. Also, schools, other community organizations, and legislators must create an environment that is more conducive to the safety of our youngsters.

In later chapters, we'll explore some specific, practical steps that can be taken to effect such protection. Before we get to any detailed solutions, however, it's important to understand more about the full scope of the problem we face with child sexual abuse and exploitation. Specifically, that means taking a closer look at child pornography and prostitution.

Pornography

When children disappear, one terrifying thing that may happen to them is that they may become subjects of pornographic films and photographs.

Much pornographic material, including pamphlets, movies, and still photographs, is produced in the United States and features American youngsters. Then, it's sent overseas for production and distribution around the world.

Finally, in the vicious, sordid cycle, the "finished" pornography often comes back in through Scandinavian countries, particularly Denmark. U.S. Customs officials have testified that children between one and thirteen years of age are featured in about 60 percent of the pornographic material that arrives in New York from overseas.

Our Senate subcommittee investigations have revealed that most pornography arrives in the United States through the mail. And there is a virtual flood of it that reaches our shores—more than 247,000 pieces in a recent four-year period, most of it involving children.

Probably, there's plenty more that slips through undetected. The Customs Service stops and opens sealed mail only when officials have reasonable cause to suspect that contraband or items subject to duties are enclosed. Factors that may lead a Customs official to check further on mail include its size, its weight, the feel of the envelope, and the origin of the letter.

When you reduce the problem of child pornography to the personal level, the impact can be even more disturbing. One ten-year-old girl was persuaded by a family friend and neighbor to pose for pornographic pictures. Years later, the pictures surfaced when the "family friend" was charged with operating a pornography ring from prison. Unfortunately, the young girl seems to have suffered almost as much as the pornographer. The following edited account comes from a letter that I received from her and read into the Senate record during a subcommittee hearing.

"My story begins one month before I graduated from high school, three months before my eighteenth birthday. An old family friend was arrested. Not long after that, I was labeled a victim of child pornography. Since that time, I have been treated with nothing but contempt and disrespect, first by the police department and then the FBI.

"Some examples: I receive a subpoena to the prosecuting

attorney's office. The detective spends an hour and a half with me trying to get information. . . .

"In the courtroom before a grand jury, I am asked to identify myself in pictures. After I do, the attorney passes the pictures around to the grand jury while I am sitting on the stand. . . .

"An FBI agent calls and says that he is coming to my home. I wait several hours, only to find that [he's] brought the wrong pictures. They are of someone else, and [he says he's] sorry.

"On several occasions, I've been threatened with prison for not cooperating. But not once has anyone expressed any concern for my well-being which, over the past year, has been hampered by violent nightmares.

"Tell me, Mrs. Hawkins, is this usual treatment for a victim of child pornography?"

One Customs official, Charles Koczka, testified at a New York hearing that child pornography will continue unless a program to control it "starts at the top—the White House and the attorney general—and unless this problem is identified as a problem."

A child may also get involved in pornography through the unwitting participation by his parents in a bogus beauty contest. For example:

A group of pedophiles may put an ad in a local newspaper asking for entrants "between the ages of 5 and 7 for a child beauty contest." When the parents respond by sending in pictures of their children, one of the pedophiles will contact them and say, "We think your child could really be a winner. Why don't you bring her over so we can take some pictures?" Prospects are usually directed to bring the children to the advertisers' "studio."

When the parents arrive with their child, the photographer persuades them to pose the child nude—or at least semi-nude—in several postures, all quite innocent. Later, the pedophiles take nude pictures of adult men and women in explicit sexual poses, superimpose the adult pictures over those of the child, and then sell the photos to other pedophiles.

Pornography, including the use of children in any sort of obscene films or photographs, can easily overlap with other forms of child abuse. We have already seen how children who are abducted or sexually abused may be made the subjects of photographs for the perverted pleasure of the abusers or others. So, reducing child abduction and sexual abuse may help reduce the problem of child pornography. And the same can be said of the impact on child prostitution.

Child Prostitution

Prostitution and prostitution-related sex-ring activities can seem even more dangerous and terrifying than individual, random cases of such abuse. The reason? Simply, there's often more insidious power in a group of pedophiles acting together than in one perverted person acting alone.

There's even evidence that there may be a wide national network of "child predators," according to Kee MacFarlane, director of a child sexual abuse center at the Children's Institute International in Los Angeles.

MacFarlane told our Senate Subcommittee on Children, Youth, and Families that she believes "we're dealing with a conspiracy, an organized operation of child predators designed to prevent detection."

She warned that preschool facilities could be used for both the selling of children into prostitution and for child pornography.

After the disappearance of Etan Patz in New York City, the press began to focus on an organization called NAMBLA, or the North American Man-Boy Love Association.

Members of NAMBLA reportedly believe that sexual relations between men and boys should be a victimless crime. As one former member of the organization said, "I think basically we're part of a whole movement of sexual liberation. I don't think the age of consent is an important issue. The thing is that people need to be able to express themselves sexually, even young people. NAMBLA is concerned about gay kids who need to be able to express themselves. And in most of these cases, the boys are just as interested in having sex as the men are."

Governmental investigators who have looked into this organization say that there are reports of a telephone number a man can call to "get a child to order." In other words, you pay several thousand dollars, put in an order for a "seven-year-old child with red hair"—and the next day he arrives at your door.

One major study of the use of sex rings in child abuse was conducted by a researcher from the University of Pennsylvania School of Nursing and published in the *Journal of the American Psychiatric Association*. According to this investigation, several factors may be involved in pulling children into a sex-ring situation:

• The children averaged eleven years of age—a time when sexual experimentation is beginning to be a very important part of their emotional growth.

• One or more adult "leaders" were involved in the eleven sex rings that the researchers studied in the Northeast and Middle West between 1978 and 1981. The adult ringleaders, who tended to be people who were respected by the children, might include neighbors, school-bus drivers, coaches, scout leaders, grandfathers, teachers, or building managers.

• The adult leaders encouraged peer pressure to keep the kids in line.

• All the sex rings employed pornography to instruct the children in what they were supposed to do. Also, the youngsters' pictures were taken in compromising positions and used to threaten them not to go to their parents.

68

• Sometimes, children were paid for being part of the ring.

• The adult leaders all used various methods of seduction: They relied on approaches that preteens would be likely to respond to positively, such as keeping secrets from parents or getting involved in "grown-up activities," like drugs, alcohol, and sex.

• As children became more deeply involved in the rings, they often became convinced that having sex with an adult was all right. Older children, in the role of what has been called "chicken hawks," were sometimes used to recruit others. (Young boys used by men for sexual purposes are called "chickens." The older boys who recruit younger kids are the "chicken hawks.")

• The parents, by all reports, tended to be passive or permissive about allowing their children to spend a great deal of time in the company of one or more adults. Some in the study expressed concern or suspicion about the activities and relationships of their youngsters. But they were unwilling to take the initiative to investigate more fully or pull their children out before the damage had been done.

The end of this road, of course, may be full-fledged prostitution, perhaps in a notorious place like New York's Times Square. Father Bruce Ritter, founder of New York City's Covenant House, has testified in Congress and elsewhere about the disastrous ends that some children come to on our big-city streets.

He tells of one pimp who entered one of his establishments and blatantly offered five hundred dollars for any thirteen-year-old girl who wanted to become a prostitute. Father Ritter also tells of a fourteen-year-old boy who was held for weeks by an abuser in a midtown Manhattan hotel; the boy finally escaped and reached Father Ritter's protection.

But child prostitution can crop up anywhere. One fifteen-year-old girl from the Deep South seemed to have everything: loving parents, a comfortable home, and a bright future. But something was missing. Somehow, the girl felt she could not communicate with her parents. So she sought affection elsewhere.

She met a man in his late twenties, and soon was having sex with him in his apartment. But then the man began to invite his friends to have sex with the girl—and began to charge them for her services.

The girl knew that what she was doing was wrong. But she was desperately afraid of telling her parents for fear that they would reject her and throw her out. In fact, that would not have been their reaction at all.

So she took the only route she thought was open: she decided to commit suicide. Fortunately, a social worker made contact with her before she could harm herself, and the girl was reunited with her parents.

According to a 1985 *Reader's Digest* report, estimates of the number of youngsters under age sixteen who are engaged in prostitution range from tens of thousands to more than one million. The figures skyrocket to twice that number when sixteen- and seventeen-year-old boys and girls are added.

Child prostitution is often the end of a long, low road of sexual abuse. As with many other forms of child exploitation, the statistics related to prostitution are uncertain because reporting practices vary. But I'll say it again: The involvement of only one innocent youngster in these terrible practices is enough to justify our outrage and decisive action.

CHAPTER SIX

The Scope of Child Abuse

Sexual abuse and abduction are only two of the many ways that children may be exploited. Other physical abuse, such as excessive beating, is also a major problem in our society. In addition, children may be put at risk of abuse by such conditions as the presence of drugs and a variety of psychological and emotional pressures.

To understand the full scope of the threat, let's consider in more detail some of thee additional chief danger areas.

Physical Abuse

Many social workers will tell you that *everyone* is capable of physical abuse against children. But fortunately, most people have significant "coping skills" that enable them to restrain themselves before they commit real harm.

In some families, however, particularly those in which educational levels are low, there are family traditions that condone severe beatings. So, in one family in West Virginia, it was common for the father to whip his children with electrical extension cords and heavy straps, even though the whippings often drew blood.

But when a local social worker told the parents that these practices weren't acceptable—and might lead to losing their children—they were willing to change their habits.

Coping skills can also be deficient among parents who drink too much, or who are under financial pressures; these adults can more easily lose their tempers and subject children to beatings.

Physical abuse exists today on a spectrum of violence that may range from excessive discipline to homicide. For example, one woman from New York was charged with suffocating her three-month-old daughter. But that may have been only the beginning. Law enforcement investigators said that they were checking to see whether eight of her other infants and toddlers, who had also died during the past fourteen years, had been victims of abuse.

To understand the scope of this blight of physical abuse, it's helpful to think in terms of three basic questions:

■ QUESTION 1 — How many children suffer physical abuse?

That's a hard question to answer because many abuse incidents are never reported. However, the number reported—a figure many experts consider to be only the tip of the iceberg—suggests that the problem we face is staggering.

According to a study by the Child Welfare League of America, a national umbrella organization representing more than 380 family service groups, 958,590 children were abused physically in 1984. And by all indications, the problem is getting worse.

The physical attacks against children are by no means limited to the United States. We seem to be part of a worldwide pattern that puts children at risk. In an annual report issued in 1985, the National Society for the Prevention of Cruelty to Children in Great Britain revealed that physical abuse of children in England and Wales increased by 70 percent between 1979 and 1984. The society also noted that at least one child a week dies at the hands of his or her parents.

■ QUESTION 2 — Who are the abusers?

There are indications that men, and especially live-in boyfriends, are among the major abusers. A study at the University of Washington in Seattle has revealed that 80 percent of the abusers in child deaths between 1981 and 1983 were men. Typically, these men were living with poor women, mostly single mothers who couldn't afford safe day-care centers or experienced babysitters to watch over their children.

These men were not accustomed to coping with children, according to Dr. Abraham B. Bergman, who conducted the study. So they tended to get irritated or angry rather easily—and then used physical violence. The number of severe injuries of children, often brain damage caused by physical blows, increased by 69 percent between the early 1970s and the early 1980s.

The violence, of course, is not limited to natural offspring. Adoptees and foster children may also be at risk. But as with many other areas of child abuse, the system of maintaining statistics may mask the full scope of the problem.

In New York City, for example, a report in late 1985 showed that child abuse at city foster-care agencies had fallen 32 percent between 1983 and 1984. But doctors who specialize in child abuse cases immediately objected, saying that the city's reporting system is defective because abuse cases aren't counted until an investigator can identify the parent or guardian who actually victimized the child. As a result, only about one-fifth of the cases of abuse or neglect that were reported at the city's foster-care facilities were actually listed as "confirmed."

■ QUESTION 3 — When does discipline become abuse?

For example, what about such an apparently mild form of discipline as spanking?

Some societies assume that any physical discipline borders on abuse—so they prohibit it. In 1979, the Swedes passed a law saying that parents may not strike their children or treat them in any other humiliating way. Many old-fashioned Americans would say this is going too far. But still, corporal punishment is a touchy issue because spanking can easily spill over into unacceptable physical beating.

The headlines in the press reflect the quandary confronting parents and child-rearing experts:

- "Child Beatings: Question of Abuse or Discipline?"
- "Parents and Experts Split on Spanking."
- "To Spank or not to Spank."

A recent Gallup poll revealed that Americans see a failure to discipline their children as a major fault of modern parents. (Child neglect came in as the second most serious parental failing.) Specifically, 37 percent of those responding in the poll said the main fault of parents was "no discipline; parents too lenient; children have it too easy." The response "Children neglected, unattended," was the choice of 24 percent of those polled.

In light of these survey findings, it's understandable that many parents would agree with the Los Angeles School Board, which voted in 1980 to reinstate disciplinary spanking of pupils. But there's also strong feeling against spanking in other quarters. For example, corporal punishment is against the law and is sometimes even linked to child abuse in Massachusetts, the District of Columbia, and New Orleans.

In any case, spanking remains a staple of discipline in most American homes. The Family Violence Research Program at the University of New Hampshire found in a 1980 poll that 88 percent of 186 parents with children from ages five to eight spanked their children. But 50 percent of those parents said that they did so as a last resort.

Still, the dangers in spanking emerged in another finding of this survey: One-third of parents who spanked their children said they did so when they felt tired, frustrated, or "out of control." This is the point at which discipline may become abuse.

In fact, many child psychologists continue to warn that physical punishment can easily lead to child abuse. Dr. Murray A. Straus, director of the Family Violence Research Program at the University of New Hampshire, discovered in a 1976 study that both physical punishment and child abuse occurred more often among families who 1) verbally abused their children, 2) were dominated by the husband, and 3) were predisposed to marital conflicts.

Is there a conclusion? Spanking, if it is to be used at all, must be used sparingly, and only after a "cooling-off" period. When emotions are intense, physical discipline can easily get out of control—into dangerous, and even life-threatening abuse.

Drugs and Child Abuse

Abuse, delinquency, and various other tragedies of childhood often begin with certain dangerous family conditions. Among these are alcohol or narcotics abuse in the American family. It's much easier for parents under the influence of these substances to lose control and begin to abuse their children—or simply to neglect them excessively.

For example, Richard Harrington, administrator of the Metro-Dade Alcohol and Drug Abuse Program in Florida, told my Senate subcommittee that drugs are a big source of many youth problems in Dade County.

"Recent studies indicate that up to 50 percent, and possibly more, of the juveniles entering the juvenile justice system have families that have been troubled with alcohol or substance abuse," he testified.

The drug and drinking habits of the parents apparently have a direct influence on the habits of the children. Mark Fontaine, training director of the Florida Alcohol and Drug Abuse Association, cited a 1981 Florida legislature report that "5,000 of approximately 8,000 male youthful offenders, or 63 percent, [themselves] had a significant substance abuse problem."

What exactly do drug and alcohol abuse have to do with child abuse?

First of all, I can think of few forms of child exploitation or neglect that are worse than encouraging a youngster to use an addictive substance.

But there is also a direct connection between the use of drugs and other types of child abuse: "At one point, 80 percent of the chemically dependent girls in our program were victims of familial sexual abuse," reported Margi Showers, director of Residential Services of the Youth and Shelter Services in Ames, Iowa.

She noted that if her staff attempted to address the sex abuse issue first, without dealing with the problem of chemical dependency, efforts to help the girls tended to fail.

In further testimony before our Senate subcommittee, now renamed Subcommittee on Children, Family, Drugs, and Alcoholism, she said, "We believe that alcoholism and drug addiction are physiological diseases. We believe that they create dysfunctional families. We believe that sexual abuse, physical abuse, and emotional abuse are by-products of dysfunctional families. And we feel that in familial sexual abuse, it is essential that we treat the whole family."

In other words, Showers has found a linkage between some cases of sexual abuse and juvenile delinquency, drug abuse, and various deep-seated emotional problems. In most instances, one problem cannot be treated without dealing with all the others.

All the evidence seems to say: "If you want to root out child abuse, you also have to root out drug abuse!"

Conditions That Give Birth to Abuse

Child abuse doesn't exist in a vacuum. It arises from and continues to be linked to unhealthy social, economic, and psychological contexts. So, to understand the full nature of the threat to our children, it's essential to know the conditions that have given birth to various types of abuse.

■ POVERTY. Sometimes, the conditions in poor homes can be so horrendous that the poverty in itself constitutes abuse.

In one rural area, social workers were called in because cows, pigs, and other animals were living right in the home. Animal feces covered the beds and floors where the four children were spending much of their time. When the youngsters would go to school, their classmates would poke fun at them.

These conditions fostered periodic running away by one of the children and the sexual involvement of a daughter with an older man.

According to a recent federal study, about 13.8 million children were found, in 1983, to be from poor families. Also, children constitute a disproportionate share of poor people in the country: although they make up only 26.8 percent of the nation's total population, they comprise 39.2 percent of the nation's poor.

Of course, poverty in itself doesn't necessarily constitute child abuse. But many children are living at or below a subsistence level, including a lack of adequate nutrition and housing. Those youngsters and their families are certainly deprived—and they are subject to conditions that may promote frustration, marital problems and, eventually, abuse.

77

■ **DIVORCE.** About half of all marriages fail, and 1.1 million children each year become part of that growing group known as "children of divorce." Arthur Norton, a demographer for the U.S. Census Bureau, says, "At some time in their lives, 60 percent of the children in this country, or forty million children, will live in single-parent homes." Also, he notes that about 92 percent of these youngsters will be reared by their mothers.

What is the impact of this epidemic of divorce?

Many children come through relatively unscathed. But a variety of recent studies indicate that some youngsters' emotional development may be impaired.

Sometimes, of course, divorce may be inevitable. But any marital split must be considered in terms of the potentially devastating impact on the children.

■ **FIGHTING BETWEEN PARENTS.** Chronic anger, expressed openly over a period of several years, is likely to have a harmful effect on children, according to a federal study reported in June 1985 in *Developmental Psychology*. The reasons? Parental anger may explode into physical attacks on children. In addition, parental fighting creates a negative climate that can undermine children's emotional growth.

Some youngsters who are subjected to this kind of family anger lose interest in their surroundings. As a consequence, they often end up having trouble at school. These children may also become overly fearful and excessively sensitive to expressions of anger.

The "danger years" for children to be affected by such parental fighting begin at least at age two. But one study has demonstrated that even one-year-olds can sense when their parents are fighting and get upset.

A key factor in the healthy emotional development of children is their awareness that the family atmosphere is, on balance, supportive and loving. Even if parents do argue, children may develop normally if they know that their parents are emotionally available to them.

But if anger is expressed in a nonsupportive context, the results can be disastrous. One child molester, called as a witness in a Senate investigation, told Senator Arlen Specter that some of the children he molested were victims of abuse at home.

"I think it could perhaps be physical," the molester testified. "I suspect some of it was psychological."

"Are you talking about the abuse these youngsters sustained prior to the contacts with you?" Senator Specter asked.

"Yes," the molester replied.

"How do you know about that?" the senator asked. "Did they tell you about it?"

"Yes."

"What did they tell you?"

"The one boy I'm speaking of, his parents had divorced, and they were in a continuing custody fight, and he, I think, was affected by that," the molester replied.

He was referring to a boy with whom he began a four-year sexual relationship when the youngster was fifteen years old. "He is the one that I would think was perhaps more psychologically abused than physically," the molester said.

"What advice would you have?" the senator asked.

"There is one reason the boys go out on the street," the molester said. "I think they are . . . seeking affection, seeking to feel that they are wanted and not neglected."

"Do you think that they start relationships with a man like you because they're not getting sufficient attention at home?" the senator asked.

" . . . I think so, to some extent," the witness continued. "They certainly would be very reluctant to admit it, but I think some definitely were seeking that kind of attention."

Clearly, this is a complicated topic. Parents can't continually look over their shoulders or remain steeped in worry about how their children may be reacting to every little mood or angry outburst.

At the same time, I believe it's important for each parent to evaluate and monitor the general tone or atmosphere that prevails in the home. Beware if there's a fight every night, a pervasive reluctance on the part of family members to express their feelings, or a prevailing atmosphere of tension. In such circumstances, the parents may be on the road to serious psychological and even physical abuse of their children.

■ FINANCIAL INSTABILITY. Most families, of course, have financial concerns. But sometimes money worries can get so serious that they begin to trickle down into the consciousness of the children—and that can mean big emotional trouble.

For example, the farm crisis in Middle America has created emotional trouble for farm children. In a study conducted by the *Wall Street Journal*, children in Iowa and other parts of the Midwest were found to be suffering from an increasing incidence of depression, bed-wetting, youthful violence, a tendency to run away, suicide, and teenage alcoholism. There may also be an increased tendency for parents frustrated by their financial problems to lash out at the nearest target—which may be the children.

■ THE SHAME AND PRESSURE OF HAVING A PARENT WHO IS A CRIMINAL INMATE. Life is particularly hard for the approximately thirty thousand children of female prisoners.

Many of these youngsters try to hide the fact that their mothers are prisoners. They may say that their mothers are in the hospital or otherwise incapacitated. Or if they're quite young, they may worry that they themselves have done something that has caused their mothers to leave. This is a heavy burden to bear.

One youngster, who was born in prison, illustrates the worst consequences of this sort of background.

After her release from jail, his mother constantly beat him, either because she was out of control from her heavy drinking or expressing anger at one of her boyfriends. Unfortunately, it was the child who suffered the consequences.

When the boy was finally taken under the care of a social worker at age twelve, he had permanent cigarette-burn marks all over his arms, and several broken bones.

Understandably, he was full of hate. Unlike many abused children, who continue to love their parents despite the torture they've undergone, this boy said over and over, "I'd like to kill my mother. I'd really like to kill her."

According to a study in the *Wall Street Journal* (March 26, 1985), "anger and alienation, hostility toward authority, and failure in school" are common characteristics of the children of female inmates. The end of this road is often drug and alcohol abuse and juvenile delinquency.

■ AFFLUENCE. At a panel of experts sponsored by the annual meeting of the American Society for Adolescent Psychiatry in May 1984, the focus was on the special psychological problems and negative family experiences of rich children.

"The children of the wealthy suffer most from lack of parental contact" reported Dr. Charles Wahl, one of the panelists. "Their parents have bought parent surrogates: tennis pros, swimming instructors, governesses, and servants. But the one true gift you can give a child is kindness and interest."

One researcher has coined the term "affluenza" for the negative impact that a certain kind of affluent background and upbringing can have on a child. Typical symptoms of "affluenza," according to John Levy, director of the C. G. Jung Institute in San Francisco, include: lack of motivation or self-discipline; suspiciousness; guilt; low self-esteem; and boredom.

Dr. Levy said that there are three causes of this problem: 1) a hothouse environment that prevents wealthy children from grappling with the normal challenges of life; 2) the unlimited opportunity to switch interests, careers, or goals when things begin to get tough in one area; and 3) parental neglect.

Therefore, it's important for families at all levels of our society to be aware of what impact the home environment is having on the children who live there. You may think, "I don't beat my children . . . I don't abuse them . . . I give them every advantage." But that last "benefit" that you've listed may not actually be a benefit at all.

In most cases of genuine child abuse, we find ourselves dealing with a broad network of emotional and psychological threads. Psychological abuse, sexual abuse, physical beatings, drug and alcohol abuse, and criminal activity are often part of the total package that we face. All must be recognized and treated, often simultaneously.

Furthermore, it's *imperative* that we act promptly to deal with these problems. If we don't, we'll be confronted with an escalating catastrophe that will shake our society and family structure for generations to come.

One long-term study of eight hundred young people in New York's Columbia County, compiled by a research team from the University of Illinois, has revealed a kind of "chain reaction" of abuse-related factors. The study found that children who were overly aggressive at eight years of age had suffered worse punishments at home than their peaceable classmates. Also, when the aggressive children became adults, they tended to engage in more fights, abuse their wives, and punish their own children severely.

More disturbing evidence of a "chain reaction" in child abuse has emerged in the work of Kee MacFarlane, of the

Children's Institute International. She has been working with youthful child molesters—all of whom are under the age of twelve.

"I have three four-year-olds [who have molested other children], and my biggest group is girls," she testified before our Senate subcommittee.

The molesters told MacFarlane that their nightmares, which had begun when they were themselves abused, had stopped when they started abusing other children. "They can make their nightmares go away by harming someone smaller," she explained. "It makes them feel more in control."

Of course, there's nothing new about this idea of "passing on" the evil in our lives to others. The Bible says that God will visit the "iniquity of the fathers upon the children and the children's children to the third and the fourth generation." Indeed, we seem to be dealing with a somewhat similar principle with abuse. Aggressive parents beget aggressive children. Abusive parents beget abusive children.

As responsible adults, we need to take any action we can to *stop* this chain reaction of abuse and exploitation. What we are dealing with is a culture-wide phenomenon that is putting our children at unacceptable risks in an adult world with which they are incapable of coping.

But still, there are many ways to minimize these risks—as we'll see when we examine the possibilities of protection both inside and outside the American home.

CHAPTER SEVEN

Parents: Ultimate Protectors

PARENTS are always the first line of protection against child abuse, exploitation, or abduction. In fact, if parents fail to keep tabs on the whereabouts and welfare of their children, they may find it's too late by the time local or federal law enforcement officials get involved.

But this is not an easy assignment. Even parents and guardians who are fine-tuned to danger may fail to keep up their vigil. What can you as a parent do to ensure you've done everything possible to protect your child?

To answer this question, let's examine the practicalities of dealing with the two biggest threats: abduction and sexual abuse.

How to Protect Your Child from Abduction

Parents who are alert can reduce the possibility that their child will be lost—and possibly abducted. So you can and *should* prepare thoroughly. Still, even the best of intentions sometimes go awry. Even the most watchful parents and guardians may find that a youngster has slipped out from under their eyes.

My husband Gene spends a great deal of time around our grandchildren. So the likelihood increases that if anything is going to happen, it will happen to them in his presence.

On one occasion, Gene went to the local barbershop to get a haircut. He wanted companionship, and so he took our eight-year-old granddaughter and our five-year-old twin granddaughters with him.

As Gene was having his hair cut, he was keeping track of the children out of the corner of his eye. But when the barber began to dust off his neck, Gene looked around once more, and saw to his consternation that one of the twins was missing.

The barbershop was in a small shopping area, and so Gene assumed that the youngster had wandered into one of the other stores. He rushed from one to another, with the eight-year-old hanging on to him by one hand and the remaining twin grasping the other. But all to no avail.

At every place he'd ask, "Have you seen this little girl's twin sister?"

The answer was always, "No, but we'll help you."

Soon, everybody in that shopping area was looking in back rooms and behind empty boxes for the little girl. But still, the missing twin was nowhere to be found.

In a calmer moment, Gene might have been heartened by the sensitivity of all those shopkeepers helping him find his missing granddaughter. But now he had no time for such thoughts. He was getting more and more worried the longer it took to locate her.

He began to wonder, "If she's not in the shopping area, then somebody must have taken her!" It was a short step from that kind of thinking to total panic.

Finally, Gene decided he'd better get on the road and start looking along the sidewalks for the youngster. So he ran over to his car with the other two children in tow, opened the door—and found all his prayers and wishes answered in that instant. When he looked in the back seat, there was the other twin lying peacefully asleep, totally oblivious to all the furor she had caused.

Gene's first reaction was incredible relief. But then, seeing the shopkeepers and their customers still looking for the youngster, he ran back to them and, store by store, announced, "I found her, I found her! She was asleep, she was asleep!"

Technically, our granddaughter was "missing," even if for only a few minutes. Certainly, she was at risk as she lay sleeping out there in that unlocked car.

But Gene, as well as many of the other business people in that area, was attuned to respond quickly and effectively to the report of a missing child. Because they acted swiftly and decisively, the chances that anything bad might have happened to our granddaughter, such as an abduction by a stranger, were greatly reduced.

Such incidents occur many times, every day, throughout our country. Usually, the ending is happy, as it was in this case for our family. But as we've already seen, sometimes the final result is pure tragedy. So, it's important for parents to act quickly and thoroughly to protect their children from becoming, even for a short time, one of the "missing."

What specific steps can you take to protect your youngster from abduction?

First of all, you should instruct your youngsters generally about what is expected of them. You might say:

• If you get separated from your parents in a shopping center, don't wander around looking for them. Go immediately to the checkout counter or the cash register. Tell the person in charge that you have lost your mom or dad and you need help in finding them.

• Never go places alone. Always try to have one or more friends with you.

87

• Never leave your yard or play area to go to someone else's home or apartment without telling your parents first.

Also, to help your youngsters function safely in the big world, you should:

• Teach your children your home telephone number and address at the earliest possible age. We started teaching our grandson Adam his telephone number when he was two years old. I would drill him with questions like:

"What's your phone number?"

"Who's your mother?"

"Who's your father?"

You can turn this kind of drill into a game, and the result can be invaluable if your youngster gets separated from you.

• Teach children "backup" telephone numbers, such as those of close friends or relatives who might be able to help them if they're unable to reach you. In addition, have them memorize 911, the local all-purpose police number.

• When your children are away from home for any reason, give them enough change to make a telephone call. The change should be *precise*: if it takes a quarter to make a call, they should have a quarter, and preferably two or three. This way, they can get in touch with you by going to a pay phone.

• It's also helpful to instruct children, even at a very young age, in making collect calls. In many places you can make collect calls locally, within the same city. So if your children *don't* have the right change, they'd still be able to get in touch with you.

Your protection program should also provide your children with information about the wisest ways to deal with people, including strangers, outside the home. You should tell them:

• You have a right to say *no* to whatever you may sense is wrong. (Children should also be told that they don't have to list reasons for saying no.)

88

• No one should approach you or touch you in a way that makes you feel uncomfortable. It's wrong for anyone to touch you on parts of the body covered by your bathing suit. Also, you shouldn't touch anyone else in those areas. Your body is special and private. (If anyone does, your children should immediately inform you. Also, emphasize that they have done nothing wrong if someone else touches them; the important thing is to let you know about it.)

• You should never get into a car or go anywhere with any person unless your parents have told you it's okay.

• If someone follows you on foot or in a car, stay away from that person. No matter what the person says to you, don't go near the car or talk to the people inside.

• Stay away from grown-ups and other older people who may ask you for help. They should be asking older people for help, not children. No older person should ask you for directions, about a "lost puppy," or about anything else.

• Don't believe anyone who tells you that your mother or father is in trouble and he or she will take you to them.

• No older person should ask you to keep a special secret. That's wrong. If you are asked to keep a special secret, tell your parents or teacher.

• If an older person wants to take your picture for any reason, tell your parents or teacher.

• If someone tries to grab you or take you somewhere, run away as quickly as you can and immediately begin yelling or screaming. If you can't run away, begin to kick, bite, or scratch. At the same time, yell something like "This man is trying to take me away!" or "This person is not my father (or mother)!"

So much for how you should teach your children. Additionally, of course, you should continually monitor their activities:

• Watch for changes in behavior. Any unusual attitude may be a signal that you should sit down and talk to your youngster about what's causing the changes.

• Teach your children to trust their own intuitions. If they sense something (or somebody) is wrong or even if they have serious doubts about something, they should be encouraged to hold off any action until they consult with you.

• Encourage your children to share their fears with you and be supportive in any discussions about those fears.

Next, know where your children are at all times:

• Be familiar with your children's friends and their usual "haunts" or the places where they're most likely to spend their after-school time. It's important to have a list of addresses and phone numbers of your children's friends so you can get in touch quickly if the need arises.

• Be alert to any teenager or adult who seems to be paying an unusual amount of attention to your children. It's especially significant—a real danger sign—if this third party gives your children inappropriate gifts.

Finally, as part of any complete protective plan, you should keep two additional considerations in mind:

Be careful about your choice of babysitters. Check their backgrounds and consult other adults who know something about them. Interview the babysitters in depth and lay down a definite set of guidelines about how you want them to watch over your children in different situations.

Also, you might occasionally arrive home unannounced, when the babysitter is not expecting you to arrive. If you don't like what you see, get rid of the individual immediately!

Sometimes, a babysitter will take a child, apparently to fulfill misguided maternal instincts.

For example, in Texas a thirty-nine-year-old woman answered a newspaper ad for a babysitter which had been placed by the mother of a three-month-old baby girl named Mallory. On her very first day of work, however, the sitter took off with the child.

After a frantic local search, the mother contacted the National Center for Missing and Exploited Children. The Center, in turn, distributed the baby's photograph, which the mother had provided, to various news media outlets and other organizations.

Mallory's picture soon appeared on ABC's *Good Morning America*. A few hours later, a woman from Houston called the National Center's hotline to report the child was with a friend who was trying to pass the youngster off as her own baby—though she had not been pregnant.

The FBI then became involved. From photographs and descriptions, the law enforcement officials knew that Mallory's outstanding identifying marks were a noticeable blood vessel on the bridge of her nose; deep dimples; and a cowlick at the center of her forehead. All this information was essential in establishing a definite identification.

Upon their arrival at the abductor's home, the FBI agents learned from the woman that her estranged husband had taken the baby to his parents in Tampa, Florida. She had convinced the man, from whom she had been separated for several months, that the baby was his.

The FBI in Texas notified the FBI office in Florida, and the shocked husband was confronted with the facts. Mother and daughter were reunited exactly one month after the abduction had taken place.

In a public place, restraining devices can be effective. Toddlers and preschoolers can be out of your sight like a shot, even if you turn your head away only for a few seconds. So, restraining devices can be helpful.

For example, there's a harness-like apparatus, sold in many child-care stores, which can be attached to supermarket shopping carts. This product keeps children from climbing out of the seats provided on those carts.

Also, there's a so-called child leash that was frequently

used in the past and is increasingly being used by concerned parents today. Obviously, you don't want to keep the child on a leash all the time. But I seriously doubt that any lasting psychological harm results from putting children in a restraining device. And a leash can do wonders for your sense of security when you and your youngster are in crowded public places.

While walking recently through a New York park, I saw a woman walking along with a preschooler who was attached to a leash. I went over and asked her where she bought it. "I didn't know they made these anymore!" I exclaimed.

"I went to my local shoemaker and asked him to make one for me," she replied. "I wore one when I was a little girl."

"What does your son think about it?" I asked.

"It doesn't bother him at all," she replied. "It gives him great freedom. He can run around as much as he needs to run around, yet I always have hold of the other end. As you might imagine, this arrangement certainly makes me feel better."

Following these various suggestions will certainly go a long way toward helping you protect your child. But sometimes, all the prior planning and preparation in the world won't do the job.

What to Do if Your Child Is Missing

If you believe your child is missing, it's critical that you act *immediately*.

First of all, if you think he may still be around the house, search it! Check closets, piles of laundry, beds (both under the covers and under the bed), inside old refrigerators or inside boxes. Look into every nook and cranny where a youngster the size of yours could crawl and hide.

Children go through phases when they like to hide from adults, probably because of a deep-rooted need to exercise some control over their little lives. You may just find that your youngster is leading you on a wild-goose chase—and believe me, that will be more a source of relief than anger when you finally find him. He may even have fallen asleep in his hiding place.

If you don't succeed in finding him inside the house, then check immediately with neighbors. If you're still unsuccessful—and certainly you should allow no more than fifteen minutes to elapse during this preliminary search—then telephone the police.

If your youngster disappears while you and he are away from home, say on a shopping trip, notify the manager and other employees in the store. Also, ask for help from other customers and bystanders in finding your child. Remember the way my husband mobilized all those people in that shopping area to look for our granddaughter?

If you do have to call the police, identify yourself and your location and say, "Please send an officer. I want to report a missing child."

You should also give your child's name, the date of birth, height, weight, and any special identifying features, such as braces on the teeth or eyeglasses.

You should also tell police the precise time you noticed the disappearance of your child, where you last saw her, and what clothing she was wearing.

Then, after you've reported your child missing, listen to the police instructions and respond fully to their questions.

You should be aware, by the way, that police will tend to respond more readily to your plight if your child is under thirteen years of age, mentally incapacitated or drug dependent, or the circumstances are such that the child may be in physical danger.

In any case, you should request that local police enter the necessary information immediately into the National Crime Information Center (NCIC) Missing Persons File. You are entitled to this service under the Missing Children

Act of 1982. Furthermore, you can go directly to the FBI and get them to verify the entry of your child's name if you have any doubts about whether or not the local police have done so.

If you find that your child's name has *not* been entered in the file, ask the FBI to do it for you. You have this right under the law. By having your child's name on this NCIC list, you'll know that any law enforcement agency in the country will have access to identifying information if the youngster is found in another community.

Also, I would strongly recommend that you contact the missing children's information clearinghouse in your state (listed in the Appendix under State Clearinghouses). These clearinghouses are established by state legislatures to assist in the investigation of missing and exploited children, and may make referrals to other appropriate organizations. The Appendix also lists organizations that provide services on the national level, as well as local and regional support groups. Frankly, I think if one of my loved ones were missing, I would get in touch with several of these groups to enlist their aid.

How can you increase the possibility that your child will be returned safely if he is missing? One way is to prepare ahead of time by knowing and keeping certain key facts and documents you can quickly put your hands on.

Here are some precautions I've come up with from my own Senate investigations and from the work of the National Center for Missing and Exploited Children.

■ **PRECAUTION 1:** *Keep a complete written description of your child.* This description should include the color of hair, color of eyes, height, weight, and date of birth. Also, you should list other identifying factors, such as eyeglasses or contact lenses, braces on teeth, pierced ears, birthmarks, and other distinctive physical attributes.

■ **PRECAUTION 2:** *Take color photographs of your child every six months.* The photographs should be of high quality and in sharp focus so the youngster is easily recognizable. It's best to have head and shoulder portraits taken from different angles so that the child's facial features are obvious.

■ **PRECAUTION 3:** *Each day, note what your child wears to school.* One of the first things the police ask when children are missing is what were they wearing. Yet it's amazing how many parents can't remember if their child was wearing a red or a blue shirt. Remembering such details is especially hard when children are old enough to dress themselves.

I'd suggest that you get in the habit of writing down this information each day on a notepad as your youngster leaves for school. When you're in the middle of the hassle of getting them out of the door so they'll get to school on time, it's difficult to focus on what they're wearing. But committing the information to paper can help.

Typically, a kidnapped youngster will tend to wear the same clothes for several days after he's abducted. So a description of his clothing can be a key factor in his safe return.

Include descriptions about any possessions your child may have when he leaves the house. Do you know what color and make your child's bike is? Does he usually carry a lunch box or schoolbag of any type?

■ **PRECAUTION 4:** *If possible, make a videotape of your child.* With the spread of videocassette recorders, you should consider making a videotape of your child in various poses and activities. Companies that offer this service are springing up all over the country. We've had this done with two of our grandchildren.

What use can you make of a videotape? Obviously, it's not possible to circulate a videotape of your child very widely. But suppose witnesses appear who claim to have seen the child somewhere. Their identification can be

95

nailed down with greater certainty if they can look at a film showing the child moving about in real-life situations. As with still photographs, however, it's important to update the videotape shots frequently—and that means every six months, if possible.

■ **PRECAUTION 5:** *Arrange with your local police department to have your child fingerprinted.* The police have trained personnel to take the prints, and they will usually be cooperative in setting up an appointment. They will give you the fingerprint card but will *not* keep a record of your child's print.

Recently, new techniques of fingerprinting have been developed so that the procedure is less messy. Therefore, you needn't hesitate just because your child is a toddler.

■ **PRECAUTION 6:** *Know where your child's general medical records are located.* Medical records—and especially x-rays—can be invaluable in helping to identify a child. You should check with your pediatrician to learn where these records are located and how you can obtain them in a hurry if the need arises.

■ **PRECAUTION 7:** *Be sure your dentist has current dental charts for your youngster.* These charts should be updated each time the dentist performs an examination or does dental work. If you move, take a copy of the dental records, including x-rays, with you. Keep them in your personal files until your child has undergone an examination with a new dentist.

The Telltale Signs of Sexual Abuse

If your youngster *is* missing for a time and then turns up, there is always a chance he has suffered sexual abuse. Or even if he hasn't been missing, sexual abuse is a possibility, especially if certain telltale signs appear—signs that we'll discuss shortly.

But first, a few general observations:

The possible danger of child abuse should cause us to be wary and highly protective of our children, but not paranoid. Sexual exploitation should never be confused with physical contacts that are simply genuine expressions of affection. A child who is touched and stroked by loving adults in a *respectable* way will always develop into a better, more well-adjusted person than one who is never touched at all.

But obviously, there are limits on where and how a child should be touched by an adult. When genuine, proper affection moves over into the area of sexual stimulation, then we usually encounter trouble.

A major job of parents is to teach children the difference between appropriate displays of warmth and affection and inappropriate sexual encounters. Of course, the younger children are, the less able they will be to understand the full implications of a sexual encounter. But if you have taken steps to ensure that your children are willing to talk with you freely, chances are you'll hear about any sex abuse right at the beginning of the problem.

Child molesting is often a repeat crime, and many youngsters are victimized several times. But if they feel free to talk the first time they become victims—and parents are alert to the problem and ready to take action—the abuse can be stopped, and sometimes before it really begins.

But if your child, for whatever reason, has failed to confide in you, you have to look for other signals. Some of the most important, according to a variety of experts in this field, include:

• Significant changes in behavior, extreme mood swings, withdrawal, unusual fearfulness, or excessive crying. If your child has typically been outgoing and talkative, for instance, but then becomes sullen, morose, or introverted, that's a signal that something is wrong.

• Bed-wetting, nightmares, fear of going to bed, or other sleep disturbances.

• Pain, itching, bleeding, fluid, or rawness in the private areas.

• Inappropriate sexual activity or an unusual interest in sexual matters. If your child seems obsessed with certain types of sexual concerns or uses sexual language that seems far too advanced for ordinary playground chatter, those could be danger signals.

• Unusually aggressive or rebellious behavior, or an unusual "acting out" of feelings.

• A fear of certain places, people, or activities. It's especially significant if a child doesn't want to be alone with certain people—including relatives. Suppose your child says, "I don't want to go to Uncle Bill's house." If that's an attitude that recurs every time you want to go to Uncle Bill's, then your child is trying to tell you something. You should sit down and ask, "Why don't you tell me why you feel that way? And certainly, you don't have to go to Uncle Bill's if you don't want to."

• An unusual reluctance to go to school. Most children will complain on many mornings, "I don't want to go to school today!" But usually, when they have gotten up, gotten dressed, and have had a little breakfast, they are eager to get started with their day.

However, the child who resists you every step of the way may be trying to avoid something at school. One of my own children was unusually reluctant to go to school during one part of her early years, and we found out later that her teacher was not being very nice to her. There was no abuse involved, but the woman came across as rather mean. She never smiled, and that bothered my youngster, who was accustomed to a cheerful atmosphere.

Our daughter actually started getting physically ill, and it was at that point we decided to change schools. The positive change in her attitude and health was dramatic!

What to Do about Sexual Abuse

First, remember two "negative" essentials:

• *Don't panic or overreact to the information disclosed by your child.* That will just frighten the youngster and may cause him to tell you less than you need to know. Remember: it's likely that your child may sense that he has done something wrong, even though from an adult perspective there's no justification for this feeling. You have to do everything in your power to counteract these feelings of shame and guilt.

• *Don't criticize your child.* If he has violated previous instructions you've given him, perhaps the worst thing you can do is to express anger.

You'll recall the basic rules for safety that we listed a few pages back. Your child may have learned those rules by rote. But when faced with a real-life situation, he simply may not have had the maturity to apply them properly.

The temptation may be to shout, "I told you not to go into anyone's home!" or to scream, "How many times have I told you not to give strangers directions!" But that will just make matters worse. And your ability to help your youngster may be irreparably damaged.

Now, consider these positive guidelines:

• *Do respect your child's privacy.* Take him to a private room or place where he can relate his story. Be careful not to discuss the incidents in front of people who don't need to know what happened. At a very young age, and certainly by age five or six, most children become very self-conscious about certain things. If your youngster thinks there's any chance he has been a "bad boy," he may be willing to talk to you but he may *not* be willing to talk in the presence of anybody else.

• *Do support your child's decision to tell the story.* It's normal for children to fear telling others about sexual abuse, and there's a special reluctance to talk to parents. So keep repeating that the youngster's decision to tell you what hap-

99

pened was the right thing to do. Also, give assurances that you'll protect him from future harm. Remember that many times a child molester will threaten a child that bad things will happen either to the child or to his parents if anybody ever finds out about the incident.

No matter how confident a youngster may seem, that veneer of self-assurance is thin indeed. Underneath, every child is deeply fearful of punishment or the loss of a parent's love.

• *Do show affection.* It's important to express your love for your youngster with words and gestures. In this regard, choose your verbal approaches to your youngster carefully.

Avoid challenging questions, especially those starting with the word "why." For example, don't say, "Why didn't you tell me this before!" or "Why did you let this happen?" That sort of opener will merely make your child defensive—and, again, may make her reluctant to tell you the whole story.

One important way to show affection is to convey positive messages in the way you talk. For example, you might say, "I'm proud of you for telling me this." Or maybe, "I'm glad it wasn't worse." Or, "I know you couldn't help this." Or most important of all, "I love you so much!"

• *Do explain to your child that he has done no wrong.* Your child may well be plagued by feelings of guilt, even though he can't quite put a finger on what the problem is. There may just be a vague sense that, "I'm responsible for this."

It's up to you to cut into these feelings and assure your youngster that he is not to blame. Although most children are enticed or tricked into acts of exploitation, they may think they should have been smarter or stronger. It's up to you to point out how the adult was unfair and evil, and how your youngster really could never have helped himself.

• *Do remember that children seldom lie about acts of sexual exploitation.* These incidents are really too disturbing to make up. As a result, you can almost always rely on your child's honesty when he reports an incident of sexual abuse. Just make the assumption that he is being truthful with you. Then, you'll be more likely to convey the impression that you believe what he has told you—and the youngster will feel freer to tell all.

• *Do keep lines of communication open with your child.* Many times, a child doesn't tell the whole story the first time around. She may forget, as a consequence of the phenomenon of "childhood amnesia." Or she may think some particular detail of the incident was unimportant. She may even be testing you with a part of the story, just to see how you'll react.

If your youngster can see that you're sympathetic, understanding, supportive and optimistic, she'll be much more likely to make additional disclosures. Even more important, she'll tend to discuss her deepest feelings and reactions to the incident.

After investigating and evaluating the possibility that child abuse has taken place, you may well determine that your child has been victimized. If that's your conclusion, what should you do? The National Center for Missing and Exploited Children, relying on congressional studies and extensive experience with abused children, suggests these three steps:

■ STEP 1 — If you think your child has been physically injured, seek out appropriate medical attention. Remember: often we do not realize that a child who has been sexually exploited is also physically injured. So don't guess. Let the professionals make an independent judgment about treatment.

■ STEP 2 — Contact the local child protection society, youth service, child abuse agency, or other appropriate social services organization. The police, sheriff's office, or other law enforcement branch should also be notified. Addresses of a number of helpful groups may also be found in the Appendix of this book.

■ STEP 3 — Strongly consider the need for counseling or therapy for your child. Ignoring the incident isn't going to help your youngster deal with exploitation. You can't simply act as though it didn't happen.

In deciding which counselor to use, look for someone who is experienced in cases of sexual victimization. One way to find a suitable therapist is to seek referrals from physicians, lawyers, and agency officials. Also, you might call one or more of the appropriate organizations in the Appendix and ask for the name of a competent professional.

Choosing a Day-Care Facility

As day-care facilities proliferate around the country, parents are becoming increasingly concerned about how well their children are treated in such places. Unfortunately, some of their worries may be well-founded because of the real possibility of neglect and even abuse.

The Department of Health and Human Services has reported that there were 7 million children in day-care arrangements in 1981. Of that number, 5.1 million were being cared for in private homes other than their own, and 1.9 million were enrolled in organized day-care centers.

I have already told you something about my early concerns and struggles to find a proper day-care center for my eldest child when I was working as a secretary in the early 1950s. And in recent years I've supported the establishment of a day-care facility for workers in the U.S. Senate.

More than three hundred companies now offer some sort of child-care subsidy to make things easier on working parents. Also, a few, like Wang Laboratories and the pharmaceutical company Hoffman-LaRoche Inc., provide on-site day care. But problems still abound.

In one survey by Child Care Systems, Inc., a Pennsylvania consulting firm, half of the respondents reported they had to switch their child-care providers at least once during a one-year period. The survey also showed that child-care problems caused parents to miss, on average, eight days of work a year. Also, 39 percent of the parents had considered quitting their jobs because of such problems.

Of course, this sort of dissatisfaction is to be expected when conscientious parents put their children into the hands of surrogates. There's always the worry that a third party won't pay as much attention to your child as you would.

But still, suppose your job is so attractive that you don't want to give it up, or so necessary that you can't. You decide that *somewhere* there must be a day-care facility that will be perfect for your child. The problem is finding it. So, you are constantly on the lookout for an appropriate place, as you switch your youngster from one facility to another.

In addition to these common feelings of dissatisfaction about the way the needs of your child are being met, there are also more concrete, health-related problems. The *Journal of the American Medical Association* reported in 1984 that one study had found a higher risk of disease among young children who were in day care. In another issue of *JAMA*, centers were described as "networks" of dysentery, diarrhea, and other intestinal problems for children and parents. Child neglect, and even abuse, at these facilities is certainly a justifiable concern.

Clearly, the situation presents parents with a mine field of possible dangers. What should you look for when you are trying to choose a good facility?

Here are some safety, health, and supervisory guidelines, which combine the best thinking from my own investigations, the American Academy of Pediatrics, and various governmental agencies.

• The facility should be licensed or registered in accordance with all local regulations, and its director should have a solid educational background in early childhood studies.

• Parents should be able to visit and observe their youngsters at any time.

• The personalities of the day-care workers should be warm and friendly, and there should be enough helpers to ensure that the special needs of each child are fulfilled. Moreover, workers should be required to take yearly physical exams and tuberculosis tests.

• The physical layout should be safe. The American Academy of Pediatrics says, "Look for loose-fill cushioned surfaces beneath all climbing equipment. Buildings should have adequate heat and light as well as proper plumbing and ventilation. Stairways should be equipped with handrails children can reach. Exit doors should be clearly marked." Every center should have an alternate exit in case fire breaks out, and fire extinguishers and smoke detectors should both be provided. If the center is located above the first floor, strong screens or bars should be installed on the windows.

• The place should be clean. On a day when you're doing some close observing, check to see if attendants wash their hands frequently, especially before feeding the children. If very young children are involved, diapering surfaces should be cleaned thoroughly with an antiseptic solution.

• The facility should have ready access to medical help. Also, those employed by the center should be able to explain clearly what they will do if a medical emergency develops.

These are guidelines only. Most important of all, I think, is your *intuitive* reaction to each center.

Somehow, you might not feel quite right about the

place. In such a case, if I were you, I would tend to go with that feeling of discomfort. I'd look elsewhere.

Finally, let me reemphasize one point: it is extremely useful to be able to drop in unannounced while your child is being cared for.

Much of the neglect and child abuse that occurs in day-care centers results, I believe, because parents simply don't take the time or lack the initiative to check out facilities as completely as they should. You have a right to know exactly what kind of care you're paying for. I would urge you strongly to exercise that right to the utmost.

Clearly, there's a great deal that parents can and *must* do to protect their children from abuse, exploitation, and abduction. If parents take most of the steps that have been outlined in the foregoing pages, the chances are they'll never have to worry about the safety of their children.

But still, it always helps to have as many backup systems as possible in case something does go wrong. So now, let's consider in more depth what community, legal, and governmental tools are available for protecting your child—and what you can do to enhance this help.

CHAPTER EIGHT

Help
Beyond
the Home

THERE'S a big parade marching by, just outside your front door—a major movement, led by organizations, agencies, legislators, and private individuals who are committed to improving the safety of our nation's youngsters. What you have to do to enhance the protection of your own children and those of your neighbors is to step out and join in.

Certainly, protection should always begin in the home. But community and governmental back-up systems are also essential to make home-grown protection completely effective. In short, concerned citizens must help pass laws and promote community practices which will uphold the rights of our youngsters.

What specific steps can you as an individual take to join this parade?

There are four basic areas where you can make your voice heard and your efforts felt: the national scene; your state legislature; your local schools; and the private sector in your community. Let's take a closer look at what's going on in each area.

A National Action Plan

Many times, the average citizen, when confronted with an issue on the national level, responds, "What can I possibly do about that? After all, I'm just one person."

Individually, you may not be able to do a great deal—but there is much you can do in concert with others. That's why it's so important to recognize that there really is a major child-protection movement that can become even more influential with your participation.

You *can* have a great impact, for example, if you'll write your national governmental representatives; support private anti-child abuse organizations, such as those listed in the Appendix, with your money and volunteer efforts; and vote for national representatives who are sympathetic to the problems.

Such simple and basic political activity can contribute greatly to social change. National support for missing children's legislation—including many letters from individual citizens—encouraged Congress to pass the Missing Children Act.

Among the important child-related measures now pending in Congress are:

■ THE CHILDREN'S JUSTICE BILL — This bill would provide federal funds to encourage states to protect child abuse victims during interviews by lawyers and governmental officials and during courtroom procedures. Also, funds would be available for treatment and counseling of such victims.

■ THE CHILD PORNOGRAPHY BILL — This legislation would amend the Racketeer Influenced and Corrupt Organizations Act (RICO) to prohibit explicitly the exploitation of children through child pornography. The bill would provide for longer sentences for large-scale pornographers and would allow victims to sue for treble damages and attorney's fees.

■ **A HIGHER EDUCATION ACT AMENDMENT** — This bill would provide interdisciplinary clinical training to graduate students entering fields related to child abuse. Future lawyers, doctors, criminal justice and mental health professionals would benefit.

■ **A LATCHKEY PROGRAM** — This legislation would encourage states, using federal funds, to investigate the possibility of after-school care for "latchkey children." (These youngsters arrive home to an empty house, usually because the parent or parents are at work.)

■ **AN INTERNATIONAL CHILD ABUSE TREATY** — This measure would establish better international procedures to find and recover abducted children.

National legislation may seem to be far removed from your everyday life. But in fact, what's done on the national level can have the most personal implications.

One of the most dramatic examples of this fact is the work of the National Center for Missing and Exploited Children in Washington, D.C. The Center began its work in the fall of 1984, after funding was provided by the U.S. Justice Department's Office of Juvenile Justice and Delinquency Prevention. And the good that the Center does can perhaps best be understood if we focus on the organization's hotline.

The main purpose of the hotline is to take calls that may lead to the recovery of missing children. About five hundred or six hundred calls come in daily, and a tremendous air of excitement builds up as, piece by piece, information comes in on a particular case.

Of course, it takes many calls to get one concrete lead. Of the approximately 122,400 calls received on the Center's hotline during 1985, some 16,880 leads emerged that assisted in the return of many of the 3,168 children recovered through the Center's efforts that year.

Workers, technical advisors and hotline operators, many of whom are parents themselves, literally cry with parents when leads go nowhere—or worst of all, to the death of a child. But at the same time, they rejoice when a child who was lost is finally found.

Fortunately, celebrations are becoming more the order of the day, both at the National Center for Missing and Exploited Children and at other agencies including the National Crime Information Center. For example, 100,000 children were reported to the NCIC in 1981 as missing, *before* the passage of the Missing Children Act in 1982. In 1985, in contrast, 330,000 youngsters were reported missing—and 321,000 of them were located!

Of course, we can't credit the 1982 law for the recovery of all those children. But the Act did codify and highlight the national procedures for reporting missing children. And it is clear that the Act was a start in the right direction.

A State Action Plan

Much of the most effective action to stop child abuse and find missing children occurs on the state level. So, the passage of state legislation must loom large in any action plan to combat child exploitation.

The National Center for Missing and Exploited Children publishes a very useful booklet on how to push for state laws to protect children. Called the "Selected State Legislation" guide, this publication details specific areas where citizens and legislators are formulating laws to protect children.

■ AREA 1: MISSING CHILDREN — Finding more of the children reported missing each year remains a major problem, and state legislation can do a great deal to expedite the process.

State laws can be passed to set up clearinghouses of information on missing and exploited children. In addition, not all state and local law enforcement agencies regularly pass on information about missing children to federal data banks. States can *require* that this information be sent for national distribution to the NCIC.

Finally, because the first few hours of any investigation are so critical, state laws can require the proper authorities to report and investigate without any waiting period.

■ AREA 2: SEXUAL ABUSE AND EXPLOITATION — Many child abuse cases are not reported. To remedy this, states can broaden the categories of professions and individuals required to report—such as physicians, school employees, social workers, psychologists, or "any other person," as the state of Delaware mandates.

Follow-up procedures are necessary to ensure the continuing safety of abuse victims. To monitor the treatment of sexually abused youngsters, state legislation can require extensive, ongoing abuse reports by agencies and institutions.

Other ways that the state monitoring procedures may be improved include:

• encouraging greater sharing of information among social service agencies and law enforcement bodies;

• protecting individuals who report cases of child victimization; and

• penalizing professionals who fail to report such cases.

Some states have even provided payments for physical examinations of victims. Others have allowed juvenile courts to issue restraining orders to prevent victimization.

■ AREA 3: CRIMINAL COURT PROVISIONS — Criminal codes should be comprehensive in describing child abuse offenses—and tough in prosecuting and in preventing early release of offenders from prison.

To this end, state laws can extend the "statute of limitations" for crimes involving children. This means that abusers can be prosecuted in the relatively distant future, even if charges are not brought against them immediately.

So, if a child is abused at age seven, and there's a relatively short statute of limitations—say, three years—the abuser can only be prosecuted up until the time that the child is ten. But if the statute of limitations runs for fifteen years, then the child would have the right up to age twenty-two, or well into early adulthood, to bring charges.

Finally, state parole procedures should be set up so that offenders will not be released under circumstances that may jeopardize the welfare of the child. Among other things, parole boards might require extensive examination of abusers to see if they pose a continuing danger to children. Also, years of outpatient treatment might be required even after the offenders are released.

■ AREA 4: THE CHILD IN THE COURTROOM — As I learned as a youngster, a child victim or witness faces a particularly difficult time in the courtroom. Some procedures may subject a child to repeated interrogation and a traumatic ordeal that some have called a "second victimization."

As a five-year-old, I was on the witness stand only one day. In contrast, one youngster who was under ten years old, was on the witness stand under cross-examination for sixteen days in the course of one sex-abuse case.

"He said the worst part was walking into the courtroom and having to see the person who hurt him the most," Kee MacFarlane of the Children's Institute International said during Senate subcommittee testimony. "He did not think he was going to be able to walk to the chair. He got frozen. And then he was afraid when he got there that he would not be able to talk."

The lawyers raised their voices at him and, what was even worse, made faces at him and mocked his answers. At one point, he just broke down. He went into a back room and cried.

All this took place during the preliminary hearings of the case. The youngster would have to go through it all over again if the case went to trial before a jury.

To counter such problems, states can adopt certain courtroom procedures to make it less stressful for a child victim or witness to testify. These include such things as allowing leading questions, or those which can be answered by a "yes" or "no" and may even seem to be putting words in the child's mouth. Other measures to make testimony easier for a youngster involve the use of videotapes, the use of anatomically correct dolls, and prompt disposition of cases.

A number of interesting and difficult issues are raised by this dilemma of the child in the courtroom—and they are issues that may influence legislative decisions.

For one thing, there's a tendency in many courtrooms for defense attorneys to charge children are being "coached" in their testimony, just because they've been receiving therapy from qualified counselors.

Children who have been abused are often, quite naturally, directed into some sort of rehabilitation program. Moreover, common sense makes it unthinkable that a child should not go into such a program. Yet some defense attorneys would say that for the child's testimony to be pure and objective, the therapy should be delayed until after the case is finished.

A major problem with such arguments, of course, is that the child needs therapy immediately after the incident. If you wait months or years for a case to be finished before seeking professional help, the emotional damage to the child may be profound and permanent.

A second "child-in-the-courtroom" issue involves recent evidence suggesting there may be good reason to reject some common assumptions that the memories of children are less trustworthy than those of adults. In fact, some psychological studies—notably at Emory University and the University of California School of Medicine— have shown that children may notice and remember details of incidents that adults either ignore or forget.

In the Emory study, conducted by Ulric Neisser, a video-tape of a basketball game was shown to both adults and children. At one point, a woman carrying an umbrella appeared on the tape. Practically no adults could remember seeing her. However, 22 percent of the fourth graders interviewed, and 75 percent of the first graders, remembered seeing the woman.

Another major criticism of child witnesses is that they tend to mix their imaginations with their memories. A number of researchers, however, have suggested that adults do the same thing. The important issue seems to be whether the youngsters can distinguish between imagination and reality.

Laws differ in many states, but youngsters as old as fourteen years may have to undergo a "competency test" before they can testify in a courtroom. Because it's usually up to judges to decide whether or not to allow such testimony, state laws need concrete, specific guidelines to limit judicial subjectivity and protect the rights of children.

To reduce the pressure on child witnesses, one report from the U.S. Justice Department suggested the following:

• Limits should be placed on the number of court appearances and preliminary hearings in which a child must participate.

• Expert witnesses should be available to counter attacks by defense counsel on a child's credibility.

• The child should be provided with a comforting adult who can explain what's going on in the courtroom.

• Closed-circuit television might be used to keep the child from confronting the defendant who has abused him. Louisiana, Kentucky, Oklahoma, and Texas permit this procedure, but the Justice Department report noted that such an approach might undercut the defendant's right to "confront his accuser"—a fundamental right in Anglo-American law.

• Videotapes might be used to record the abused child's first statement to law enforcement officials. After this, the child would have to testify in court. But at least the videotape might cut down on testimony at multiple hearings and provide a clear impression of the child's reaction to the incident immediately after it occurred.

■ **AREA 5: PROTECTING THE PRIVACY OF THE CHILD VICTIM** — A child victim may face the additional ordeal of the release and publication of personal information, including the child's name, the family address, and the details of the assault. Such publicity is not only embarrassing for the child and the family, but it may also result in severe psychological and emotional harm. What can state laws do about this? Among other things, they can penalize those who reveal the child's identity and provide for strict privacy for any documents that lead to identification.

■ **AREA 6: SCHOOLS** — Schools are often a good place to teach youngsters about child abuse, exploitation, and abduction. State-approved classroom materials and curricula can help greatly in the educational process.

Laws may also require that lists of missing children be circulated at schools and compared with lists of enrolled students to help identify victims of abduction and kidnapping. In addition, channels should be established to inform schools about the arrest of any school employees who have been charged with sexual or other child-related offenses.

■ **AREA 7: LICENSING AND CRIMINAL HISTORY INFORMATION** — People who are in regular contact with children as part of their employment should be checked for a possible criminal record. Many state laws require such a check. Those covered by such a requirement would include employees and volunteers who are involved in school systems, youth service organizations, and day-care centers.

A two-process check through the law enforcement system and federal agencies should cost between $20 and $25 per individual. Obviously, the total cost for a given state will vary, according to the number of people to be checked. But identifying possible child molesters is certainly worth the cost.

■ **AREA 8: TRAINING FOR PROFESSIONALS WHO WORK WITH CHILD VICTIMS** — People who work regularly with child victims must be trained for the special demands of this responsibility. States can mandate educational programs for all professionals in this field, including social service and law enforcement investigators, and even prosecutors and judges.

■ **AREA 9: TREATMENT AND REHABILITATION OF THE CHILD VICTIM** — It's expensive to treat children who have been the victims of sexual assault, incest, child molestation, and other crimes. They need medical treatment, counseling, and other forms of professional help to give them the opportunity to have a normal childhood. State laws may provide for such assistance, and may even require that the person convicted of an assault or abuse should pay for the treatment and rehabilitation of his victim.

■ **AREA 10: COURT-APPOINTED ADVOCATES** — State laws can ensure that children who are victims of crimes will have the support and protection of a court-appointed advocate. In the past, such advocates have been appointed by courts to serve only children who have been abandoned, abused, or neglected. But your state can include all forms of child exploitation. In addition, the laws may permit the advocate to be a trained lay person rather than an attorney.

■ **AREA 11: PARENTAL KIDNAPPING** — One of the most difficult problems faced by any justice system is parental kidnapping, when an estranged spouse who does not have custody of the child is the abductor. Despite the fact that a parent is involved, these abducted children are still seriously at risk, and they often become the victims of physical and emotional abuse.

Most states have tried to deal with this problem by

making parental kidnapping a felony. In addition, state legislation has been used to broaden the felony charge to include those who merely conceal children. Those who assist the parent in kidnapping the child may also be subject to a felony charge.

■ **AREA 12: CHILD PORNOGRAPHY AND CHILD PROSTITUTION** — One way the state laws can protect children against child pornography is to require photography processors to report any instances they encounter of child pornography. Also, the laws may provide that any use of children in pornographic pictures, regardless of the commercial use of those pictures, is a crime.

States can also act against child prostitution by making the act of hiring a child prostitute a special, extra-serious criminal offense. Legislation may also be enacted to provide penalties for parents or guardians who permit their children to engage in prostitution.

Obviously, a great deal more could be said on each of these topics. And a great deal more *has* been written. If you'd like a copy of a complete state legislation package, contact:

National Center for Missing and Exploited Children
State Legislation
1835 K Street, N.W., Suite 700
Washington, D.C. 20006

By now you can see there's a lot going on toward improving state laws in the area of child protection. What's your next step?

An individual's best bet is to link up with one of the many organizations, such as some of those listed in the Appendix, who are actually advocating changes in child-protection legislation. Obviously, letters or other proposals in the name of a group carry more weight than those in the name of an individual.

Child advocacy organizations propose bills to legislators, monitor the legislative process, and lobby for the bill's passage.

A great ally in any legislative effort is the Child Welfare League of America. Established in 1920, it acts as a consulting and training service for more than 400 public and private child welfare agencies around the country.

The League has been particularly active in promoting state legislation that focuses on the prevention of child abuse and the treatment of victims. It has also worked on the national level to establish uniform reporting systems for child abuse cases.

For further information about how you as an individual can join ranks with this group write:

Children's Campaign
c/o Child Welfare League of America
440 First Street NW
Washington, D.C. 20001

If your time and energy permit, I encourage you, as an individual, to contact your state representatives. Remember, it's helpful to submit a written proposal. If they support your idea, a written proposal puts them in a better position to act.

If your state has a two-house system of government, it is important to contact representatives from both sides of your legislature. Also, speak with members from both parties; laws to protect children transcend party affiliations. As we've seen in my Senate experiences, bills that are cosponsored and have bipartisan support are the most likely to succeed.

A School Action Plan

School may seem a safe and secure place for your youngsters. But in fact, children are sometimes abducted from school. Also, there are many instances of child abuse by employees or other adults on school premises.

The power and influence that an individual parent can wield on a local level is significant. But you have to position yourself to take advantage of that power.

The first thing to do is join the PTA, and maybe even become an officer in some of the parent activities or associations.

I was a room mother and also a member of the PTA when my oldest child was in first grade, and I know such involvements can be a problem if both parents work. However, most parent association meetings are held at night, and that makes it easier for those with tight daytime schedules.

In any case, I think it's essential that at least one parent and preferably both attend all the meetings they can on a regular basis. In this way, you can get a feel for the competence and concern of the teachers and also a sense of the security of the physical facilities.

Some school policies you might promote include:

• An absolute rule that no child can be released without the permission of the parent or guardian of that child.

• The use of security guards in each school. As a matter of fact, I think it's a good idea to have a police officer assigned to each school.

• Comprehensive screening procedures before a child is allowed to enroll in a school. All new students should be required to submit records from former schools. Students who cannot provide such records should be asked to provide birth certificates or similar identification; meanwhile, the names of these students should routinely be submitted to federal and state agencies involved with finding missing children. In most public schools, very little information is required for a child to attend classes. As a result, a youngster who has been abducted may be placed in a school by his abductor and stay there for years without anything unusual being noticed.

In one case, an abducted boy was in a public school a

half-dozen years before the truth was learned. Most abducted children, if they survive the first few months of their kidnapping, end up in a school somewhere. They could easily be found if the screening procedures of the schools were more stringent.

The importance of having alert school officials is illustrated by an incident at a public school in Fremont, California. A child in the school complained to school personnel that she "used to have another name" and wanted her "real mommy."

The school officials contacted the National Center for Missing and Exploited Children, and found that the youngster has been abducted by her father eight months before. The police moved quickly to arrest the man, and the child was soon returned to her mother.

• Strict prohibition of drugs in school. Now, it's a federal offense for drugs to be sold within a thousand feet of any school. But local communities can make this rule even stricter—and most important of all, ensure that it is enforced.

• More concerned parents on local school boards. I've told many young parents that one of the best things they can do to protect their children at school—and to ensure the youngsters will get a good education—is to run for the local school board. Often, when policies are made at that level, they can have a tremendous impact on the way the average elementary and secondary schools go about their daily business.

• A rule that the schools should post information about missing children in a prominent place on a regular basis.

For example, two sisters, eight-year-old Brandy and four-year-old Misty, were taken from their home in Topeka, Kansas, by a couple acquainted with their mother. Two years elapsed with no sign of the two girls, but in the interim their names and pictures were distributed by the Lost Child Network, and placed on NCIC records.

As a result, a twelve-year-old girl in an Arkansas school recognized Brandy's picture on a poster, identified her to the authorities, and the girls were returned to their mother.

• The institution of a voluntary child fingerprinting program to provide participating parents with a set of their youngster's fingerprints.

Obviously, there are many ways parents can influence school policies. But the first step is to *get involved*. If you just stand on the outside and criticize, your suggestions and demands will likely just fall on deaf ears.

A Child Safety Day

This is an event that highlights the tragedy of missing children and educates the community to the problem of abduction and what can be done about it. Awareness is the essential first step in eradicating the problem. The Child Safety Day can educate both parents and children about what needs to be done.

And the program really works. In one day at Tuskegee, Alabama, 25 percent of the youth in the county were fingerprinted; even more received dental charts and were photographed. This was a total community effort, with the private business sector, local government agencies, and various volunteer groups contributing significantly.

For example, Burger King funded the fingerprinting and dental cards. The city government provided photographic equipment and supplies. The local U.S. Army Reserve unit pitched in by providing four dentists. In all, one hundred volunteers worked on the event.

Other communities that have participated in this project—to name just a few—include Visalia, California; St. Petersburg, Florida; Des Moines, Iowa; Erie, Pennsylvania; and Houston, Texas.

Typically, such an event is organized over a ten-week period. When the day finally arrives, nine "stations" are set up to educate and assist parents and children in improving their child safety situation. Here's a brief summary of how the concept works:

■ **STATION I: WELCOME** — Approximately three volunteers welcome parents and children. They distribute the basic materials needed for the day and assure the parents that any records that are made will remain in the parents' possession *only*.

■ **STATION II: VITAL STATISTICS** — Six volunteers at this station compile the information needed by investigating officers when a child is reported missing.

■ **STATION III: HEIGHT AND WEIGHT** — Although this is the slowest moving station, having an accurate reading on a youngster's height and weight is critical information for the first stage in any search for a missing child. Three volunteers usually handle this spot.

■ **STATION IV: DENTAL** — Volunteer dentists and others from the dental community chart children's teeth at this location. As a general rule, one dentist will be required per hour for twenty children.

■ **STATION V: PHOTO** — Using an "instant" camera, a frontal photo is taken of the child here and attached by volunteers to the vital statistics form. Usually, handling fifteen children per camera per hour requires about six volunteers.

■ **STATION VI: FINGERPRINTING** — Here, uniformed officers or other highly trained volunteers explain to children the process of fingerprinting—and then they take the prints. It's important to convince youngsters that the procedure will be painless, and also, if ink is used, that it will wash off.

■ **STATION VII: CLEAN UP** — Approximately three volunteer firefighters explain the various rescue techniques used in searching for a lost child or helping one involved in an accident. The firemen also give the children safety tips and go over fire prevention rules.

■ **STATION VIII: SAFETY** — Approximately three volunteer firefighters explain the various rescue techniques used in searching for a lost child or helping one involved in an accident. The firemen also give the children safety tips and go over fire preventon rules.

■ **STATION IX: OUTSIDE ACTIVITIES** — At this spot, police volunteers can provide, on an informal basis, information about how fingerprints are used in police work. The officers can also help put identification marks on bicycles, toys, and other articles owned by the children. In addition, it's a good idea to provide some sort of entertainment here to complete the atmosphere of a family outing.

Obviously, this summary just provides a brief overview of how to stage one of these events. I suggest checking the Appendix for those organizations that provide more complete information on conducting Child Safety Days.

Parents and children, who will both be attending this event, will see in graphic but upbeat terms what can and must be done to protect our youngsters. Also, they'll see that they're by no means alone. The presence of so many friendly and helpful firefighters, police, medical professionals, and business representatives has to increase anyone's sense of comfort and support.

The victimization of children is a horrible thing. But it's the small, unrepresentative minority in our society who hurt or abduct our youngsters. Most adults want the best for any child—and it's important that your child understands that.

Epilogue

Joanne Simpson, who had recently been divorced, was a single parent. But her pretty, bright four-year-old daughter, Hope, was all a mother could hope for: a comfort in times of loneliness, a daily source of joy and good humor.

The mother and daughter made their home in Phoenix, but when Hope caught pneumonia, Joanne was told by a local hospital that she needed certain identification papers, obtainable only in the city where they had previously lived, to get proper treatment for the child. So she decided to leave the little girl with a friend, Sarah, whom she had known for a few months. (I am changing the names.)

As it turned out, that was a mistake. When Joanne arrived back in Phoenix from out of town a few days later, the babysitter was gone and so was Hope.

That was December 1980, before the passage of the Missing Children Act and the heightened awareness in the nation about the plight of abducted and exploited youngsters. But Joanne immediately launched her own personal investigation, criss-crossing the country and searching through all but eleven states to find Hope. She notified local police authorities; contacted the FBI; even made up her own identification fliers on Hope and distributed them along every major roadway that she traveled.

But there was no response. Months and then years went by, but still there was no trace of the child.

Finally, in early 1985, Joanne contacted the newly-established National Center for Missing and Exploited Children in Washington. The Center began circulating pictures and information about Hope to a large number of organizations around the country. Finally, in January 1986, a hot lead came in from California.

A social worker called the Center and asked if a 9-year-old girl named Hope Anne—who was now living in a foster home in California with a different last name— could be the missing Simpson youngster. The experienced hotline operator knew that Hope Anne Simpson was among the Center's hundreds of abduction cases. She immediately turned the information over to one of the Center's technical advisors.

The advisor first confirmed that the case had been entered in the FBI's National Crime Information Center files. After further inquiry, the advisor determined that the Hope Anne in California was indeed the Hope Anne Simpson who had been abducted five years before in Phoenix.

The National Center arranged to give the child's mother and grandfather round-trip airplane tickets to California through the World Airways "Operation Homeward Bound" program. They also received complementary accommodations from Quality Inns International, which participates in programs to help reunite separated families.

At their first meeting, both Joanne Simpson and her daughter immediately recognized each other, and the five-year saga of the mother's search for her missing child ended with a tearful reunion and a heartfelt vow: "I'm never letting you go again!"

What had happened to Hope Anne in those intervening years?

The memories of young children may be fragmented and distorted by selective childhood amnesia, which blocks out unpleasant experiences. But Hope, a strong-minded youngster with an extraordinary will to survive, held on to important memories. She persevered in her desire to be reunited with her mother, no matter how difficult the pressures she faced during the long separation.

The girl remembered, for example, that her mother, who liked to drive a pickup truck, used a distinctive nickname on her citizen-band radio. Sometimes, it seemed such memories were Hope's only contact with love. During the two years she was in the company of her abductor, she was often beaten.

"One time she put me in a cold shower and I jumped out and bit her," the girl said.

The woman allegedly told the girl that her mother had died, but Hope said, "I didn't believe her because my mother said she would never leave me."

Finally, the abductor abandoned the girl in a Los Angeles motel. The motel manager, who noticed her, telephoned the police.

Hope was then put into the custody of the California Social Services System, and was shuffled through several foster homes. It was a bad experience, she recalled: "I hated it. Too many drug addicts."

One year before she was found, Hope was almost adopted. But she knew if this happened, she might never be reunited with her real mother, so she refused to accept the adoption.

Many child-care officials didn't believe Hope when she insisted she had been taken away from her mother. But one social worker, Bill Thomas, began to listen. There was a ring of truth in what the girl was saying, and he wanted to know more.

He encouraged her to talk out her memories of her family, and some of her recollections convinced him that she was telling the truth. At that point, he decided to check with the National Center—and the stage was set for the long-sought reunion.

The case of Hope Anne Simpson is the other, brighter side of the Adam Walsh tragedy. Unfortunately, far too many missing children either never are found—or turn up dead or far more seriously abused than Hope.

John Walsh understands this all too well. "If children have been missing for five years, they're usually not found alive," he said, commenting upon the Hope Simpson case.

But still, with the new national agencies and search mechanisms in place, the more positive stories are increasing in number. And the more the average citizen learns about the national investigative tools that are available, the more children we can save. As we improve our legislation, local community awareness, and parental safety measures, we can expect the worst risks to decline dramatically. The classic happy ending should become not only what we can wish for with all our hearts, but also what we can expect with greater and greater confidence.

APPENDIX

This appendix describes organizations that assist missing and exploited children and their families, as well as organizations and agencies that work for legislative improvements in the areas of child abuse and exploitation. Although there are many local grassroots programs concerned with these issues, only nonprofit or public programs currently in operation at the state, regional, or national level are included here.

This appendix was compiled from information provided by the National Center for Missing and Exploited Children. The inclusion of a program, organization, or resource does not constitute an endorsement or certification of it by the National Center and should not be taken as such. The National Center does not have regional, state, or local branch offices. Organizations bearing a name similar to the National Center for Missing and Exploited Children are not official agents of the National Center.

About the National Center for Missing and Exploited Children

The National Center for Missing and Exploited Children serves as a clearinghouse of information on missing or exploited children; provides technical assistance to citizens and law-enforcement agencies; offers training programs to schools and law-enforcement agencies; distributes photos and descriptions of missing children nationwide; and provides information and advice on effective state legislation to ensure the safety and protection of children.

Appendix

A toll-free telephone line is open for those who have information that could lead to the location and recovery of a missing child:

1-800-843-5678

The TDD hotline (for the deaf) is:

1-800-826-7653

The fifteen toll-free hotlines cover Canada as well as the United States. Because these calls can literally be a matter of life or death, the National Center asks that the hotline number be used only by those individuals who have critical information to report.

Anyone who is seeking information about the problems of missing and exploited children should write to:

National Center for
Missing and Exploited Children
1835 K Street, N.W., Suite 700
Washington, D.C. 20006

How to Use This Appendix

Programs are listed under three categories, National Organizations, State Clearinghouses, and State and Regional Organizations, based on each program's primary function and scope of activity. National programs offer information and provide services on a national scale. State Clearinghouses are established by state legislatures to assist in the investigation of missing and exploited children, and may make referrals to appropriate organizations.

Those programs listed by State and Region are primarily support services and resource centers for a state or region. Most of the agencies categorized by state accept calls from outside their immediate areas, offer assistance, and make referrals to other agencies. Additionally, a number of organizations are able to tap resources on a national level.

The services offered by the state and regional programs are classified into the following categories. It is important to note, however, that although one or more of these categories may appear under the service headings, all services described in these definitions may not be offered.

Appendix

■ **ABDUCTION BY UNKNOWN INDIVIDUAL:** The program specifically handles cases involving abduction of a child by an individual unknown to the victim.

■ **COURT MONITORING:** The program provides support to victims and their families during the trials of their accused offenders. The court watch program monitors sentences assigned to offenders.

■ **CULT GROUPS:** The program specifically handles cases involving children in cult groups and provides support and counseling to victims and their families upon a child's return home.

■ **FAMILY SERVICES:** The program provides immediate action in the event that a child is missing, such as gathering necessary information, making posters, referral to appropriate agencies or authorities, emotional support, and victim and family counseling.

■ **FAMILY VICTIM FUND:** The program assists in coordinating efforts to raise funds for families of missing children.

■ **IDENTIFICATION KITS:** The program provides information packets to aid parents in assembling identifying information on their children that would be essential in the search for a missing child.

■ **INFORMATION CLEARINGHOUSE:** The program collects and disseminates information on all aspects of missing and exploited children and may make referrals to appropriate agencies.

■ **LEGISLATIVE ADVOCATE:** The program actively supports and works to improve current legislation concerning missing and exploited children.

■ **NEWSLETTER:** The program produces and distributes (or makes available on request) a newsletter containing preventive and educational information and/or missing children information.

■ **PARENTAL ABDUCTION:** The program specifically handles cases involving abduction of a child by a noncustodial parent.

■ **POSTER/PICTURE:** The program distributes posters and/or pictures of missing children through local or national networks.

■ **PREVENTION/EDUCATION:** The program has available instructional materials concerned with the prevention of child abuse, exploitation, and safety (literature, cassettes, slides, videos, etc.); provides speakers for civic organizations; and conducts outreach and public awareness activities (community child safety days, etc.).

■ **RESOURCE HANDBOOK:** The program produces and distributes (or makes available on request) a publication listing available resources and support groups concerning missing and exploited children.

■ **RUNAWAYS:** The program specifically handles cases involving children who are voluntarily missing.

■ **SEARCH TEAM:** Volunteers are available to aid in the coordination and execution of the search for a missing child.

■ **SEXUAL EXPLOITATION COUNSELING:** Trained counselors are available to victims of sexual exploitation and their families.

A "Comment" heading is added to those programs requiring specific information not included in the definitions above.

NATIONAL ORGANIZATIONS

American Humane Association
9725 East Hampden Avenue
Denver, CO 80231

(303) 695-0811

The American Humane Association offers expertise, technical assistance, training, advocacy, and information on child welfare, child protection, and related areas. Although American Humane has published legislative analyses and has been involved in legislative advocacy, its efforts are now directed more toward continuing the compilation of national statistics on intrafamily child abuse and neglect and toward training of child welfare personnel and technical assistance to involved agencies.

Child Find, Inc.
P.O. Box 277
New Paltz, NY 12501

(914) 255-1848
(800) 426-5678

7 Innis Avenue
New Paltz, 12561

Child Find registers missing children, whether they are runaways or victims of stranger abduction or parental abduction. The program provides counseling for runaways who call on the toll-free line and refers them to appropriate agencies.

Appendix

Child Welfare League of America
440 First Street, N.W.
Washington, D.C. 20001

(202) 638-2952

The league acts as a consulting and training service for more than four hundred public and private child welfare agencies around the country. It has been particularly active in promoting state legislation focusing on the prevention of child abuse and the treatment of victims, and has worked on the national level to establish uniform reporting systems for child abuse cases.

Childkeyppers International
P.O. Box 6456
Lake Worth, FL 33466

(305) 586-6695

Parents are provided with complete assistance in cases of stranger abduction, noncustodial parental kidnapping, and voluntary disappearance. Childkeyppers International provides full education programs, classroom teaching, safety posters, and runaway prevention as well as seminars for organizations. The project staff provides counseling for parents and works with siblings when a child is murdered or missing. Key Connector, a child crisis line, is operated for adolescents in need of help or information. Childkeyppers also operates a twenty-four-hour telephone line and will accept collect calls. Legal assistance is provided on an emergency basis, and the program assists law enforcement with statistics, in tracking the dead, and in searching for and recovering missing children.

Children's Rights of America, Inc.
2069 Indian Rocks Road, Suite B
Largo, FL 33544

(813) 593-0090
(813) 584-0888 (twenty-four-hour hotline)
(800) 237-5200 (U.S.A. sighting hotline)

The program operates a twenty-four-hour hotline, a U.S.A. sighting hotline, provides active counseling for parents involved in a missing child or child abduction case, and makes referrals for child abuse and exploitation cases. Individualized case assistance for registered parents includes consultation with their attorneys regarding interstate child custody laws, coordination of investigation, and follow-up after recovery of the child. The program actively solicits photographs of missing children for dissemination to the media nationwide. They will, upon request, recommend reasonably priced attorneys and investigators nationwide who have an effective record in missing children cases. The program has contacts in India, Canada, England, and other countries.

Council of State Governments
P.O. Box 11910
Iron Works Pike
Lexington, KY 40578

(606) 252-2291

The Council of State Governments is a nonprofit, state-supported service organization of all fifty states and the U.S. territories. The council collects and distributes information, promotes interstate cooperation, and works to improve state administration and management on both a national and regional basis.

Find the Children
11811 West Olympic Boulevard
Los Angeles, CA 90064

(213) 477-6721

The program works directly with the media in getting photographs of missing children broadcast throughout the country. Find the Children is located in a television production office and works with KNBC-TV on Child Search, a three- to five-minute segment on a missing child that is broadcast every Monday on the 5 P.M local news around the country. The program also supplies photographs and information on missing children to newspapers, magazines, and television talk shows.

Appendix

Foundation to Find and Protect America's Children
P.O. Box 386
Wyckoff, NJ 07481

(201) 891-0049

The foundation acts as a clearinghouse for parents of missing children; disseminates pictures of missing children to the media, law enforcement, and other interested parties; promotes education and awareness; and encourages grass roots support for missing children legislation. The foundation currently works to locate missing children.

Home Run
A National Search for Missing Children
4575 Ruffner Street
San Diego, CA 92111

(619) 292-5683
(800) MISS YOU (United States)
(800) HIT HOME (California)

The program operates a twenty-four-hour hotline to be used by parents to report a child missing or by runaways or missing children to get help, acts as a liaison between runaways and their parents to encourage their reunion, and refers runaways to shelters throughout the country. Information on missing children is entered into the program's computer for later use and for sharing with other involved agencies (national network of resources, food, shelter, clothing, medical attention, and transportation). The program works either to speed children home or, when this is not advisable, to send them where they will receive care and protection. Children returning home are provided transportation if necessary.

Appendix

Juvenile Justice Clearinghouse
National Criminal Justice Reference Service
P.O. Box 6000
Rockville, MD 20850

(301) 251-5500
(800) 638-8736

The clearinghouse, as part of the National Criminal Justice Reference Service, maintains, and will access on request, a data base containing information and research on all juvenile justice issues, including missing children and child exploitation. The data base includes, but is not a comprehensive source of, state and federal legislation and related materials. The clearinghouse also provides information on current programs, policy issues, and other areas and can refer callers to other sources.

Kid Watch
292 Hoffman Lane
Hauppauge, NY 11788

(516) 582-8444
(800) KID WATCH

Executive Offices:
American Child Protective Association, Inc.
521 Fifth Avenue
New York, NY 10017
The national Kid Watch computer holds pertinent information on members. A national action plan is executed immediately when a missing child is reported.

The Lost Child Network
8900 State Line Road
Suite 351
Leewood, KS 66206

(913) 649-6723
(800) 843-5678 (for sightings)

The program's main focus is to place photographs of missing children on the photo-processing envelopes of three corporations. Accompanying the pictures are descriptive information about the children and the 1-800 telephone number for sightings provided by the National Center for Missing and Exploited Children in Washington, D.C. Through the efforts of these three companies, the photographs will be distributed to photography stores, major food store chains, national drugstore chains, national department stores, military bases, and major discount store chains throughout the United States and Canada at a rate of approximately forty-two million per year.

The Missing Children Network
2211 South Dixie Drive
Dayton, OH 45409

(513) 298-8134
(800) 235-3535

The network distributes photographs of missing children through a nonprofit network of organizations and a television network of over ninety local stations throughout the country, free of charge. The network operates a toll-free hotline to collect sighting information, offer assistance, and make referrals to appropriate agencies.

National Association of Counsel for Children
1205 Oneida Street
Denver, CO 80220

(303) 321-3963

The association, which serves attorneys representing children, guardians *ad litem*, juvenile court judges, and other advocates of children, has expertise in legislative developments in the states and litigation related to such areas as child abuse, child protection, children's rights, child prostitution and pornography, and child custody disputes. The association publishes a newsletter with a section on state legislation, has assisted in the development of relevant state laws, and can make referrals to members throughout the country with expertise on specific legal issues.

Appendix

National Child Safety Counsel
4065 Page Avenue
Jackson, MI 49204

(517) 764-6070

The National Child Safety Council is the oldest and largest federal tax-exempt 501(C)(3) nonprofit child safety organization in the United States. It is funded entirely by private contributions. The council has a thirty-year history of saving young lives by providing safety education materials to law-enforcement agencies and schools. In addition, the council prints the Abducted Children Directory, a service of Missing Children Search, which is distributed every three months to the FBI and state and local law-enforcement departments throughout the country.

National Clearinghouse on Child Abuse and Neglect Information
U.S. Department of Health and Human Services
P.O. Box 1182
Washington, D.C. 20013

(202) 251-5157

The clearinghouse is a national resource for information on all aspects of child abuse and child neglect, including medical neglect of handicapped infants and abuse in out-of-home day-care facilities. The clearinghouse disseminates model child protection legislation developed by the National Center on Child Abuse and Neglect and maintains a searchable data base available through DIALOG Information Services that contains, among other materials, portions of state laws relevant to child protection, child exploitation, and related issues. The clearinghouse distributes several analyses based upon its collection. Bibliographies, custom searches, documents, and referrals are available.

Appendix

National Coalition for Children's Justice
2998 Shelburne Road
Shelburne, VT 05482

(802) 985-8458

The National Coalition for Children's Justice is a private, non-profit, tax-exempt organization dedicated to improving protective services for children and creating public awareness of the many social injustices inflicted upon the young. The coalition has provided research data to many congressional committees, produces preventive education materials, and is working to establish a national child victim network that will coordinate and disseminate information on known sex criminals as well as on missing children believed to have been forced into prostitution or cult activity.

National Committee for the Prevention of Child Abuse
322 South Michigan Avenue, Suite 1250
Chicago, IL 60604-4357

(312) 663-3520

The National Committee works for the prevention of child abuse and child neglect through state and national public awareness programs, a network of state chapters, and through advocacy and information dissemination. The National Committee supports, with the efforts of the National Child Abuse Coalition, an advocate in Washington, D.C., who tracks state child abuse legislation and lobbies for and monitors federal child abuse legislation. The National Committee publishes a newsletter and a variety of information materials on child abuse, child neglect, and related issues.

National Conference of State Legislatures
1125 17th Street, Suite 1500
Denver, CO 80202

(303) 292-6600

The National Conference of State Legislatures is a nonpartisan organization that provides a wide range of services to the nation's 7,500 state legislatures and their staffs. Its Children and Youth

Program produces publications, responds to requests for information, conducts research, and provides technical assistance and seminars on child support and child welfare reform.

National Council of Juvenile and Family Court Judges
P.O. Box 8970
Reno, NV 89507

(702) 784-6012

The National Council, through its training arm, the National College of Juvenile Justice, provides membership services and training for judges and others involved in juvenile and family courts. Areas of interest include child support enforcement, permanency planning, and child advocacy. The council's research arm, the National Center for Juvenile Justice, collects and analyzes juvenile court data and conducts statutory analyses in such areas as confidentiality, fingerprinting of juvenile offenders, waiver, and transfer. The council publishes a newsletter, a quarterly journal, and a monthly digest of juvenile court decisions.

National Crime Prevention Council
805 15th Street, N.W.
Washington, D.C. 20036

(202) 393-7141

The council works with the Advertising Council to produce a national public service advertising campaign to reduce crime and to promote crime prevention; disseminates materials to state and local groups; provides technical assistance; and focuses on the protection of children and youths.

National District Attorneys Association
1033 North Fairfax Street, Suite 200
Alexandria, VA 22314

(703) 549-9222

The association serves the nation's prosecution attorneys and works to improve the administration of justice through educational and informational programs for its members. The association prepares amicus briefs to assist the court, conducts surveys of prosecuting attorneys, awards scholarships to prosecuting attorneys, and publishes a variety of educational and resource materials, including a national directory of prosecuting attorneys. The association has information and expertise on juvenile justice, juvenile delinquency, child welfare, and the prosecution of child sexual offenders, and can make referrals through its committees and its membership.

National Fingerprint Center for Missing Children
P.O. Box 945
Kirksville, MO 63501

(816) 627-1277

The center provides fingerprinting supplies and information, crime prevention materials, public service advertisements, window decals, and metal reflective road signs for use in local programs. The road signs read "Our Children Have Been Fingerprinted for Identification." Fingerprints are classified, and palm prints are analyzed for clarity by professionally trained classifiers. This central, independent facility for computerized search and recovery assistance helps law enforcement agencies, on parental request, to identify missing children nationwide. There is a one-time fee of $3.50 per card to register a child's fingerprint card at the center. Upon notification, vital information is placed into the National Crime Information Center (NCIC) computer network by law enforcement officers. Technical assistance is provided free of charge to communities and organizations that are interested in beginning a fingerprinting program.

National Governors Association
444 North Capitol Street, N.W.
Washington, D.C. 20001

(202) 624-5300

The National Governors Association, founded in 1908, represents the governors of the fifty states, the Commonwealth of Puerto Rico and the Northern Mariana Islands, and the territories of the Virgin Islands, Guam, and American Samoa. Its missions are to influence the shaping and implementation of national policy and to apply creative leadership to the solution of state problems. The association's operations are supported by member jurisdictions, and its policies and programs are formulated by the governors.

National Legal Resources Center
for Child Advocacy and Protection
American Bar Association
1800 M Street, N.W.
Washington, D.C. 20036

(202) 331-2250

The Legal Resources Center provides technical assistance, consulting, and training on legal issues related to child welfare and child protection. The center, through these activities and through dissemination of publications and analyses, promotes the reform of child welfare laws and administrative and judicial procedures. The center produces publications and has expertise in the areas of parental kidnapping, missing children, and child sexual and criminal exploitation.

National Network of Runaway and Youth Services
905 6th Street, S.W., Suite 411
Washington, D.C. 20024

(202) 488-0739

This resource network for runaway shelters, community programs, and coalitions dealing with the concerns of runaways and youths acts as an information clearinghouse, sponsors educational programs, and promotes policies and programs to help runaways and youths.

National Organization for Victim Assistance (NOVA)
1757 Park Road, N.W.
Washington, D.C. 20010

(202) 393-6682
(202) 232-8560

NOVA offers technical assistance, referrals, and information in support of victims' assistance programs and victims' rights, and recently established a child victimization committee. NOVA tracks victim-related state legislation and publishes a directory of legislation that reviews and gives citations for state laws related to victim rights and services. The directory includes some model pieces of legislation and new legislative developments relevant to child sexual assault and exploitation. NOVA also publishes a victim-service program directory.

National Victim Resource Center
633 Indiana Avenue, N.W., Suite 1342
Washington, D.C. 20531

(202) 724-6134

The center is a national clearinghouse of information on victim assistance and compensation and relevant legislation, programs, and organizations. A computerized data base of state laws concerning victimization includes some legislation on child victims of sexual assault and sexual exploitation, as well as videotaping of child victims for use in legal proceedings. The file tracks pending as well as enacted legislation, and includes citations and summaries. The center also maintains a computerized file of descriptions of national victim assistance programs.

Parents of Murdered Children
1739 Bella Vista
Cincinnati, OH 45237

(513) 242-8025
(513) 721-5683

This self-help organization, through its forty-one chapters and two hundred contact persons, assists parents of murdered children and survivors of victims of crime.

Appendix

Washington Victim Witness Service
2366 Eastlake Avenue, East
Suite 311
Seattle, Washington 98102

(206) 322-0658

Prevention, education, and general victim witness services.

Appendix

STATE CLEARINGHOUSES

Alabama Department of Public
  Safety
Missing Children Bureau
P.O. Box 1511
Montgomery, AL 36192
(205) 261-4207
(800) 228-7688 in state

Arizona Department of Public
  Safety
Criminal Intelligence Research
  Unit
P.O. Box 6638
Phoenix, AZ 85005
(602) 262-8469

Arkansas Attorney General's
  Office
Missing Children's Services
  Program
201 East Markham Street,
  Suite 510
Heritage West
Little Rock, AR 72201
(501) 371-2007

California State Department of
  Public Safety
Missing/Unidentified Unit
P.O. Box 13417
Sacramento, CA 92813
(916) 739-3845

Colorado Bureau of
  Investigation
Missing Children
  Clearinghouse
2002 Colorado Boulevard
Denver, CO 80222
(303) 759-1100

Connecticut State Police
Missing Persons Division
290 Colony Street
Meriden, CT 06450
(203) 238-6575
(800) 367-5678 in state
  and
Connecticut Department of
  Public Safety
Division of State Police
100 Washington Street
Hartford, CT 06793
(203) 566-4240

Delaware State Police
State Bureau of Investigation
P.O. Box 430
Dover, DE 19903
(302) 736-5873

Florida Department of Law
Enforcement
Missing Children
Clearinghouse
P.O. Box 1489
Tallahassee, FL 32302
(904) 488-5224

Georgia Bureau of
Investigation
Intelligence Section
3121 Panthersville Road
Decatur, GA 30037
(404) 244-2554

Illinois State Police
I-SEARCH
200 Armory Building
Springfield, IL 62706
(217) 782-5227
(217) 782-6429
(800) 843-5763 in state

Iowa Department of Public
Safety
Wallace State Office Building
Des Moines, IA 50322
(515) 281-6278
(515) 281-8422

Kansas Bureau of Investigation
Statistical Analysis
1620 Tyler Avenue
Topeka, KS 66604
(913) 232-6000

Kentucky State Police
1250 Louisville Road
Frankfort, KY 40601
(502) 227-8708
and
Louisville Division of Police
Criminal Intelligence
633 West Jefferson Street
Louisville, KY 40202
(502) 589-3047
and
University of Louisville
School of Social Work
Louisville, KY 40208
(502) 588-6402
and
Family Violence Prevention
and Services
Governor's Office
Capitol Building, Room 107
Frankfort, KY 40601
(502) 564-2611
and
Victims Advocacy Division
Office of the Attorney General
Capitol Building
Frankfort, KY 40601
(502) 564-5904

Maryland State Police
Center for Missing Children
1201 Reistertown Road
Pikesville, MD 21208
(301) 653-4412
(800) 637-5437 works for out
 of state
and
Maryland State Police
Investigation Division
Investigation Headquarters
Pikesville, MD 21208
(301) 653-4433

Massachusetts State Police
Missing Persons Unit
West Grove Street
Middleboro, MA 02346
(617) 727-8972
(800) 447-5290 in state

Mississippi Highway Patrol
P.O. Box 958
Jackson, MS 39205
(601) 987-1212

Missouri State Highway Patrol
Missing Children Unit
P.O. Box 568
Jefferson City, MO 65102
(314) 751-3313

Montana Department of
 Justice
Identification Bureau
303 North Roberts Street
Helena, MT 59620
(406) 444-3817

Nevada Office of the Attorney
 General
Capitol Complex
Carson City, NV 89710
(702) 885-4170
and
Nevada Division of
 Investigation
Department of Motor
 Vehicle/Public Safety
555 Wright Way
Carson City, NV 89711
(702) 885-4408

New Hampshire State Police
Department of Public Safety
Hazen Drive
Concord, NH 03305
(603) 271-2535

New Jersey State Police
Missing Person Unit
Box 7068
West Trenton, NJ 08625
(609) 882-2000
and
Department of Law and Public
 Safety
R J Hughes Justice Complex
8th Floor, CN085
Trenton, NJ 08625
(609) 984-5830

New York State Police
Information Network
New York State Police
Building 22—State Campus
Albany, NY 12226
(518) 457-9466
and
New York State Division of
Criminal Justice Services
Executive Park Tower
Albany, NY 12203
(518) 457-6113
(518) 457-6054
and
New York State Division of
Criminal Justice Services
Bureau of Identification
Executive Park Tower/
Stuyvesant Plaza
Albany, NY 12203
(518) 457-6326
(518) 457-6050

North Carolina Center for
Missing Children and Child
Victimization
Department of Crime Control
and Public Safety
P.O. Box 27687
Raleigh, NC 27611
(919) 733-7974
(800) 552-5437 in state

Ohio Department of
Education
Missing Children's
Educational Program Office
65 South Front Street,
Room 719
Columbus, OH 43215
(614) 466-6837
(800) 325-5604 in state

Oklahoma State Bureau of
Investigation
Special Operations
P.O. Box 11497
Oklahoma City, OK 73136
(405) 682-6724

Pennsylvania State Police
Missing Persons Unit
Bureau of Criminal
Investigations
1800 Elmerton Avenue
Harrisburg, PA 17110
(717) 783-5524

Rhode Island State Police
P.O. Box 185
North Scituate, RI 02857
(401) 647-3311
(800) 544-1144 in state

South Carolina Law
 Enforcement Division
Missing Person Information
 Center
P.O. Box 21398
Columbia, SC 29221
(803) 758-6000
(800) 332-4453 in state

South Dakota Attorney
 General's Office
Division of Criminal
 Investigation
500 East Capitol Street
Pierre, SD 57501
(605) 773-4614

Tennessee Bureau of
 Investigation
P.O. Box 100940
Nashville, TN 37210-0940
(615) 741-0430

Texas Department of Public
 Safety
Crime Records Division
P.O. Box 4143
Austin, TX 78765
(512) 465-2811
(800) 346-3243 in state

Virginia State Police
Records and Statistics
P.O. Box 27472
Richmond, VA 23261
(804) 232-2000
 and
Virginia Department for
 Children

Resource Center for Missing
 and Exploited Children
805 East Broad Street
Richmond, VA 23219
(804) 786-4835
(800) 822-4453 in state

Vermont Attorney General's
 Office
Child Protection Unit
109 State Street
Montpelier, VT 05602
(802) 828-3171

Washington State Police
Missing and Unidentified Unit
P.O. Box 2527
Olympia, WA 98504
(206) 753-1650

Canada

Solicitor General of Canada
Planning and Liaison Division
Room 11F, 340 Laurier Street
 West
Ottawa, Ontario
Canada KIA oP8
(613) 991-2815

Royal Canadian Mounted
 Police Task Force
1200 Alta Vista Drive
Ottawa, Ontario
Canada KIA oR2
(613) 993-7425

Appendix

Note: Individuals may also contact the Federal Bureau of Investigation and the Office of Juvenile Justice and Delinquency Prevention:

Federal Bureau of
  Investigation
Department of Justice
9th Street and Pennsylvania
  Avenue, N.W.
Washington, D.C. 20535
(202) 324-5050

Office of Juvenile Justice and
  Delinquency Prevention
Department of Justice
633 Indiana Avenue, N.W.
Washington, D.C. 20531
(202) 724-5940

Appendix

STATE AND REGIONAL ORGANIZATIONS

Alaska

Alaska Youth Advocates, Inc.
135 North Park Street
Anchorage, AK 99508
(907) 274-6541 (twenty-four hours)
(907) 563-SAFE (shelter)

Services: Prevention/Education; Family Services; Runaways

Comment: The program operates a shelter for runaways eleven to seventeen years of age and a message service for runaways and their parents. It also provides two training programs for youths to develop skills for effective social interaction and to develop communications and problem-solving skills for building on family strengths. Services are confidential and immediate.

Child S.A.F.E.
8612-2 Boundary Road
Anchorage, AK 99504
(907) 333-6405

Services: Prevention/Education; Family Services; Identification Kits; Legislative Advocate; Sexual Exploitation Counseling

Appendix

Missing Children of America, Inc.
P.O. Box 10-1938
Anchorage, AK 99510
(907) 248-7300
(907) 688-4011

Services: Prevention/Education; Family Services; Poster/Picture; Identification Kits; Legislative Advocate; Parental Abduction; Abduction by Unknown Individual; Runaways

Comment: The organization works with law enforcement agencies, child abuse groups, and social workers to determine the causes and effects of child disappearance and is willing to share its extensive experience in locating missing children abroad.

Arizona

Hide and Seek Foundation, Inc.
P.O. Box 56363
Phoenix, AZ 85079
(602) 433-1028

Services: Prevention/Education; Family Services; Poster/Picture; Parental Abduction; Abduction by Unknown Individual; Runaways; Search Team

Comment: The foundation coordinates search efforts in individual cases and offers crisis counseling and advice on a twenty-four-hour helpline. Staff members teach proper and legal methods of searching for missing children. All search coordinating is done by the national office (see p. 180) through the Missing Children Network (see p. 138). The foundation has affiliated chapters across the country.

Appendix

Operation Child Identification
P.O. Box 26610
Phoenix, AZ 85068
(602) 241-0456

Services: Prevention/Education; Identification Kits

Tucson Missing Children Program
900 Pima County Courts Building
111 West Congress Street
Tucson, AZ 85701
(602) 792-8411

Services: Family Services; Poster/Picture; Identification Kits; Parental Abduction; Abduction by Unknown Individual; Runaways

California

Abandoned and Runaway Children Center
428 Osage Street
Spring Valley, CA 92077
(619) 226-0206

Services: Prevention/Education

Appendix

Adam Walsh Child Resource Center
721 South Parker
Suite 280
Orange, CA 92668
(714) 547-1361

Services: Prevention/Education; Identification Kits; Legislative Advocate; Court Monitoring

Comment: The center's "Safety with Strangers" education program uses slides and audiocassettes and is designed to teach young children how to respond when approached by strangers. In the court monitoring program, trained volunteers observe trials of accused child molesters and the sentencing of convicted molesters. These data are used to make judicial and legislative changes. Parents of missing children are provided with information about what they should do in their search for their children. The center does not refer private investigators and has no investigators on its staff. The center has affiliated chapters across the country.

The American Missing Childrens' Foundation
P.O. Box 590473
San Francisco, CA 94159
(415) 863-6555

Services: Prevention/Education; Family Services; Poster/Picture; Identification Kits; Abduction by Unknown Individual; Legislative Advocate; Search Team

Comment: The foundation handles cases of abduction by unknown individuals only.

California Child Abduction
Child Abduction Recovery and Enforcement Council
1950 Sunset Street, Suite 200
San Bernardino, CA 92415
(714) 383-3631
Services: Family Services

Comment: A service of the District Attorney's Office.

The Child Assault Prevention Training Center
1727 Martin Luther King, Jr. Way, Suite 108
Oakland, CA 94612
(415) 893-0413
Services: Prevention/Education

Friends of Child Find
741 East Street, #257
Woodland, CA 95695
(916) 662-2389

Services: Prevention/Education; Family Services; Poster/Picture;
Identification Kits

Comment: The program also provides a community alert program.

K.I.D.S., Inc.
Kare Information Dedication Solution, Inc.
P.O. Box 8208
Palm Springs, CA 92263
(619) 320-1188
Services: Prevention/Education

Appendix

Laura Bradbury Organization
P.O. Box 2712
19086 Magnolia Avenue
Huntington Beach, CA 92646
(714) 963-6356

Services: Prevention/Education

Missing Children's Project
1084 Avon Avenue
San Leandro, CA 94579
(415) 352-6883

Services: Prevention/Education; Family Services; Poster/Picture; Identification Kits; Resource Handbook

Missing Children's Resource Center
2404 Broadway
San Diego, CA 92102
(619) 235-4459

Services: Prevention/Education; Family Services; Parental Abduction; Abduction by Unknown Individual

Orange County Search and Rescue
P.O. Box 5548
Buena Park, CA 90622
(714) 828-3200

Services: Prevention/Education; Family Services; Identification Kits

Comment: The program founded the National Kid Print Program which is completely compatible with the format used by the National Crime Information Center (NCIC) computer. Volunteers are trained by FBI technicians in fingerprint techniques.

Our Children
P.O. Box 364
Yucaipa, CA 92399
(714) 797-5982

Services: Prevention/Education

Protect Your Child
P.O. Box 414
San Lorenzo, CA 94580
(415) 276-2350

Services: Parental Abduction; Runaways

Top Priority: Children
P.O. Box 2161
Palm Springs, CA 92263
(619) 323-1559

Services: Prevention/Education; Poster/Picture; Identification Kits; Newsletter; Legislative Advocate

Vanished Children's Alliance
P.O. Box 2052
Los Gatos, CA 95031
(408) 354-3200

Services: Prevention/Education; Family Services; Poster/Picture; Identification Kits; Parental Abduction; Abduction by Unknown Individual; Runaways; Newsletter

Comment: The alliance disseminates information and pictures through the media, refers recovered children to reputable therapists, provides expert witnesses for court cases, and participates in cooperative efforts and networking with various groups around the country.

Colorado

Hide and Seek Foundation, Inc.
P.O. Box 440216
Aurora, CO 80044
(303) 680-9933

Services: Prevention/Education; Family Services; Poster/Picture; Identification Kits; Parental Abduction; Abduction by Unknown Individual; Search Team

Comment: The foundation coordinates search efforts in individual cases and offers crisis counseling and advice on a twenty-four-hour helpline. Staff members teach proper and legal methods of searching for missing children. All search coordinating is done by the national office (see p. 180) through the Missing Children Network (see p. 138). The foundation has affiliated chapters across the country.

S.T.O.C.
Stop Taking Our Children
8720 East Colfax Avenue
Denver, CO 80220
(303) 798-1824
(303) 331-0923

Services: Prevention/Education; Family Services; Identification Kits; Parental Abduction; Abduction by Unknown Individual; Runaways; Legislative Advocate

Comment: The program operates a twenty-four-hour hotline and directs parents through the legal system.

Appendix

District of Columbia

Missing Children of Greater Washington
4200 Wisconsin Avenue, N.W., Suite 201
Washington, D.C. 20016
(202) 686-1791

Services: Prevention/Education; Family Services

Sasha Bruce Youth Work
1022 Maryland Avenue, N.E.
Washington, D.C. 20002
(202) 546-4900
(202) 546-6807

Services: Runaways

Florida

Adam Walsh Child Resource Center
501 East South Street
Orlando, FL 32801
(305) 423-2326
  and
1876 North University Drive, Suite 306
Fort Lauderdale, FL 33322
(305) 475-4847

Services: Prevention/Education; Identification Kits; Legislative Advocate; Court Monitoring

Appendix

Comment: The center's "Safety with Strangers" education program uses slides and audiocassettes and is designed to teach young children how to respond when approached by strangers. In the court monitoring program, trained volunteers observe trials of accused child molesters and the sentencing of convicted molesters. These data are used to make judicial and legislative changes. Parents of missing children are provided with information about what they should do in their search for their children. The center does not refer private investigators and has no investigators on its staff. The center has affiliated chapters across the country.

Dee Scofield Awareness Program, Inc.
4418 Bay Court Avenue
Tampa, FL 33611
(813) 839-5025

Services: Prevention/Education; Family Services; Poster/Picture; Identification Kits; Parental Abduction; Abduction by Unknown Individual; Runaways

Comment: The program also produces and disseminates information on specific missing children cases, legislation, evaluation of police and other public officials, and guidance on citizen involvement. Contacts are located in Canada, England, Germany, Saudi Arabia, and Lebanon.

Missing Children Center, Inc.
750 West Highway 434
Winter Springs, FL 32708
(305) 695-4357

Services: Prevention/Education; Family Services

Missing Children Help Center
410 Ware Boulevard, Suite 400
Tampa, FL 33619
(800) 872-5437
(813) 623-5437

Services: Prevention/Education; Family Services; Poster/Picture;
Identification Kits; Parental Abduction; Abduction by Unknown
Individual; Runaways; Legislative Advocate

Switchboard of Miami, Inc.
35 Southwest Eighth Street
Miami, FL 33130
(305) 358-1640

Services: Runaways

Georgia

American Red Cross—Metro Atlanta
Missing & Exploited Children Program
1925 Monroe Drive, N.E.
Atlanta, GA 32324
(404) 296-0505
(404) 881-9800 ext. 353

Services: Prevention/Education

FIND ME, Inc.
(For Individuals Missing Everywhere)
P.O. Box 1612
La Grange, GA 30241-1612
(404) 884-7419

Services: Prevention/Education; Family Services; Resource Handbook

Comment: The program also operates an adult missing persons group.

Hawaii

S.T.O.P.
Student Training Offers Protection
777 Kapiolani Boulevard, Suite 2111
Honolulu, HI 96813
(808) 949-5577
(808) 526-3766

Services: Prevention/Education

Illinois

Friends of Melissa Ackerman
Route 34 Professional Place
P.O. Box 263
Somonauk, IL 60552
(815) 498-9245

Services: Prevention/Education

Appendix

Illinois Task Force on Parental Abduction
645 North Wood Street
Chicago, IL 60600
(312) 421-3551

Services: Prevention/Education; Parental Abduction

Protect the Children
P.O. Box 49
Steger, IL 60475
(312) 281-6779

Services: Prevention/Education; Family Services; Parental Abduction; Abduction by Unknown Individual

Indiana

S.L.A.M. of Indiana
Society's League Against Molestation
P.O. Box 1013
Greenwood, IN 46142
(317) 882-5497

Services: Family Services

Comment: The program has affiliated chapters across the country.

Iowa

Project: Missing Children
515 Locust Avenue
Carter Lake, IA 51510
(712) 347-6674

Services: Prevention/Education; Family Services; Poster/Picture; Parental Abduction; Abduction by Unknown Individual; Runaways

Appendix

Kansas

The Kansas Missing Children Foundation
3427 Elmwood Road
Wichita, KS 67218
(316) 687-6083
(316) 682-4693

Services: Prevention/Education; Family Services; Poster/Picture; Identification Kits; Parental Abduction; Abduction by Unknown Individual; Information Clearinghouse

Kentucky

E.C.H.O.
Exploited Children's Help Organization
720 West Jefferson Street
Louisville, KY 40202
(502) 585-3246

Services: Prevention/Education; Family Services; Parental Abduction; Abduction by Unknown Individual; Runaways; Sexual Exploitation Counseling

Kentucky Task Force on Exploited and Missing Children
Office of the County Judge
500 West Jefferson Street, 6th Floor
Louisville, KY 40202
(502) 625-5787

Services: Prevention/Education; Parental Abduction; Abduction by Unknown Individual; Sexual Exploitation Counseling

Louisville/Jefferson County Exploited and Missing Children's Unit
400 South 6th Street, 3rd Floor
Louisville, KY 40202
(502) 588-2199

Services: Prevention/Education; Parental Abduction; Abduction by Unknown Individual; Sexual Exploitation Counseling

Comment: The unit investigates all reports of child sexual exploitation and missing youths, never closes a case until a missing child is found, holds preventive programs in the local schools, and conducts public awareness campaigns. The unit uses a model computer system for tracking and locating missing children within Jefferson County. The unit offers limited technical assistance to other jurisdictions interested in implementing their own exploited and missing children units.

Maryland

S.L.A.M.
Society's League Against Molestation
P.O. Box 833
Beltsville, MD 20705
(301) 953-3237

Services: Prevention/Education; Court Monitoring

Comment: The program has affiliated chapters across the country.

Appendix

Stephanie Roper Committee, Inc.
P.O. Box 178
Cheltenham, MD 20623
(301) 952-0063

Services: Family Services; Court Monitoring

Comment: The committee offers support to victims and their families during the trials of their accused offenders, and a court watch program monitors sentences assigned to offenders.

Massachusetts

Children's Safety Alliance, Inc.
P.O. Box 750
Wellesley, MA 02181
(617) 235-9130

Services: Prevention/Education

Find Our Lost Kids, Inc.
P.O. Box 438
Quincy, MA 02269
(617) 773-3655

Services: Prevention/Education; Family Services

New England K.I.D.S.
P.O. Box 26
West Springfield, MA 01090
(413) 732-9873
    and
516 Grafton Street
Worcester, MA 01604
(617) 791-1130
    and
4 Auburn Court
Brookline, MA 02146
(617) 791-1130

Services: Prevention/Education; Identification Kits; Resource Handbook

Comment: The program also sets up Safe Home projects in Massachusetts communities and has established a resource library.

Society for Young Victims
5 Washington Street
Manchester, MA 01944
(617) 526-1080

Services: Prevention/Education; Family Services; Poster/Picture; Identification Kits; Parental Abduction; Abduction by Unknown Individual; Runaways

Michigan

K.E.N.N.Y.
Kids Everywhere Now Need You
P.O. Box 517
Hazel Park, MI 48030
(313) 398-3560

Services: Prevention/Education; Abduction by Unknown Individual

Runaway Assistance Program
398 Park Lane
East Lansing, MI 48823
(517) 351-5757
(800) 292-4517

Services: Prevention/Education; Runaways

Comment: The program provides crisis counseling and information and referral to runaways, potential runaways, and their families. Crisis counselors are available twenty-four hours a day, seven days a week. All calls are confidential, and callers may remain anonymous.

Minnesota

Missing Children–Minnesota
2951 Aldridge Avenue, North
Minneapolis, MN 55411
(612) 522-4549

Services: Prevention/Education; Family Services; Poster/Picture; Identification Kits; Parental Abduction; Abduction by Unknown Individual; Runaways; Legislative Advocate

Missouri

Child Find–Missouri
P.O. Box 19823
St. Louis, MO 63144
(314) 781-8226

Services: Prevention/Education; Family Services; Poster/Picture;
Legislative Advocate; Parental Abduction; Abduction by Unknown
Individual; Runaways

Comment: The program maintains a list of agencies and support
groups for referral of cases and advises parents on how legally to
regain their children in the case of parental abduction.

Synergy House
P.O. Box 12181
Parkville, MO 64152
(816) 741-8700

Services: Runaways

Montana

Friends of Child Find–Montana
737 South Billings Boulevard, No. Zero
Billings, MT 59101
(406) 259-6999

Services: Prevention/Education; Family Services; Poster/Picture;
Identification Kits; Parental Abduction; Abduction by Unknown
Individual; Runaways

Nebraska

Project: Missing Children
P.O. Box 19025
Omaha, NE 68119
(402) 345-0969

Services: Prevention/Education; Family Services; Poster/Picture;
Parental Abduction; Abduction by Unknown Individual; Runaways

Comment: The program distributes pictures and fliers to law enforcement agencies and the media nationwide. Staff monitor current legislation and make referrals to local resources.

Nevada

Community, Runaway and Youth Services
190 East Liberty
Reno, NV 89501
(603) 323-6296

Services: Family Services; Poster/Picture; Runaways

Comment: The program disseminates photographs of missing children to other runaway and homeless youth programs across the country. It also provides information to the parents regarding the procedures for filing a missing persons report, the function of law enforcement agencies in these cases, and the existence of services of other organizations.

Nevada Child Seekers
P.O. Box 42368
Las Vegas, NV 89116
(702) 388-7333

Services: Prevention/Education; Family Services; Poster/Picture; Runaways

New Hampshire

New Hampshire Network for Runaways and Homeless Youth
P.O. Box 440
Manchester, NH 03015
(603) 668-1920

Services: Prevention/Education; Family Services; Poster/Picture; Runaways

New Jersey

Bergen County Sheriff's Office
Missing Person's Bureau
1 Court Street
Hackensack, NJ 07601
(201) 646-2192

Services: Prevention/Education; Family Services; Identification Kits; Parental Abduction; Abduction by Unknown Individual; Runaways

Essex County Sheriff's Office
Missing Person's Unit
County Courts Building
Nelson Place
Newark, NJ 07102
(201) 621-4111
(201) 621-4178

Services: Prevention/Education; Identification Kits

K.I.D.
Kids in Danger
P.O. Box 1063
Island Heights, NJ 08732
(609) 693-1203

Services: Prevention/Education; Family Services; Poster/Picture;
Runaways

Morris County Prosecutor's Office
Missing Person's Unit
Hall of Records
Morristown, NJ 07960
(201) 829-8159
(201) 829-8550 (evenings)

Services: Prevention/Education; Parental Abduction; Abduction by
Unknown Individual; Runaways

Comment: The program enters information into the National
Crime Information Center (NCIC) computer.

Appendix

New Jersey Commission on Missing Persons
Department of Law and Public Safety
25 Market Street, CN 085
Trenton, NJ 08625
(609) 984-5830

Services: Legislative Advocate; Information Clearinghouse

Comment: The commission has the use of the state police to assist in cases of missing persons. Upon request, the commission will provide training to agencies starting missing and exploited children units.

Ocean County Commission on Exploited and Missing Children
146 Chestnut Street
Toms River, NJ 08753
(201) 349-1454

Services: Prevention/Education; Information Clearinghouse

Comment: The commission enters all appropriate missing person information into the National Crime Information Center (NCIC) computer and assists in the training of all county law enforcement officers with respect to prevention of child abduction and exploitation.

Services for the Missing
150 Berlin Road
Gibbsboro, NJ 08026
(609) 783-3101

Services: Prevention/Education; Family Services; Parental Abduction; Abduction by Unknown Individual; Runaways; Legislative Advocate; Search Team

New York

Adam Walsh Child Resource Center
249 Highland Avenue
Rochester, NY 14620
(716) 461-1000

Services: Prevention/Education; Identification Kits; Legislative Advocate; Court Monitoring

Comment: The center's "Safety with Strangers" education program uses slides and audiocassettes and is designed to teach young children how to respond when approached by strangers. In the court monitoring program, trained volunteers observe trials of accused child molesters and the sentencing of convicted molesters. These data are used to make judicial and legislative changes. Parents of missing children are provided with information about what they should do in their search for their children. The center does not refer private investigators and has no investigators on its staff. The center has affiliated chapters across the country.

Center for Missing Children, Inc.
P.O. Box 10088
Rochester, NY 14610
(716) 473-2389

Services: Prevention/Education; Family Services

Child W.A.T.C.H.
(Why Aren't the Children Home?)
P.O. Box 732
Elmira, NY 14901
(607) 732-0562

Services: Prevention/Education; Family Services; Identification Kits; Legislative Advocate

Comment: The program's fingerprinting system is administered by police officers and parent volunteers; parents keep the fingerprint cards.

Children in Crisis
401 Broadway, Suite 1603
New York, NY 10013
(212) 334-9161

Services: Prevention/Education; Family Services; Abduction by Unknown Individual; Runaways; Cult Groups

Children's Rights of New York, Inc.
19 Maple Avenue
Stony Brook, NY 11790
(516) 751-7840

Services: Prevention/Education; Family Services; Legislative Advocate; Newsletter

Comment: The program provides advice and referral services to parents involved in child-stealing disputes or missing children disputes. They maintain a list of attorneys, private investigators, and other support groups with expertise in assisting in missing children cases.

Cult Hotline and Clinic
1651 Third Avenue
New York, NY 10028
(212) 860-8533

Services: Prevention/Education; Family Services; Cult Groups

F.A.C.T.
Families Aware of Childhood Traumas
P.O. Box 99
Carle Place, NY 11514
(516) 997-6695

Services: Prevention/Education; Family Services; Poster/Picture; Parental Abduction; Abduction by Unknown Individual; Runaways; Legislative Advocate; Information Clearinghouse; Family Victim Fund

Institute for Youth Advocacy
Covenant House
460 West 41st Street
New York, NY 10036
(212) 613-0349

Services: Family Services; Runaways

Comment: Covenant House has short-term crisis shelters in New York, Toronto, and Houston that provide food, clothing, shelter, medical and legal services, educational and vocational services, and individual and family counseling to anyone under the age of twenty-one on a twenty-four-hour basis, no questions asked.

Appendix

Project F.A.C.T.
Services After Family Emergencies
Town of Babylon Youth Bureau
151 Phelps Lane
North Babylon, NY 11703
(516) 422-7200
(516) 665-3207

Services: Prevention/Education; Family Services; Runaways

Victims of Crimes Advocacy League
P.O. Box 136
Haines Falls, NY 12436
(518) 589-5778

Services: Prevention/Education

North Carolina

Find My Child Support Network
Room 627
336 Fayetteville Street Mall
Raleigh, NC 27601
(919) 833-3780

Services: Prevention/Education; Family Services

Protect-A-Child
P.O. Box 1812
Durham, NC 27702
(919) 477-3739

Services: Prevention/Education; Family Services; Identification Kits

Comment: Chapters in fourteen states.

Appendix

Reach Out Center for Missing Children
1003 Stadium Drive
Durham, NC 27704
(919) 471-3112

Services: Prevention/Education; Family Services

Ohio

Adam Walsh Child Resource Center
P.O. Box 2871
Toledo, OH 43606
(419) 531-8400

Services: Prevention/Education; Identification Kits; Legislative Advocate; Court Monitoring

Comment: The center's "Safety with Strangers" education program uses slides and audiocassettes and is designed to teach young children how to respond when approached by strangers. In the court monitoring program, trained volunteers observe trials of accused child molesters and the sentencing of convicted molesters. These data are used to make judicial and legislative changes. Parents of missing children are provided with information about what they should do in their search for their children. The center does not refer private investigators and has no investigators on its staff. The center has affiliated chapters across the country.

Friends of Child Find, Ohio
P.O. Box 37168
Maple Heights, OH 44137-0168
(216) 663-2467

Services: Prevention/Education; Identification Kits

Appendix

Lima Area Child Assault Prevention Project
799 South Main Street
Lima, OH 45804
(419) 222-1168

Services: Prevention/Education

Oklahoma

Silver Fund
6001 N.W. Expressway
Oklahoma City, OK 73132
(405) 722-2234

Services: Prevention/Education; Family Victim Fund

Oregon

Friends of Child Find of Oregon, Inc.
P.O. Box 756
Springfield, OR 97477-0131
(503) 341-3822

Services: Prevention/Education; Identification Kits

Comment: The program provides twenty-four-hour telephone service for families of missing children and for public information.
Guidelines for setting up Absentee Reporting Programs and volunteer fingerprinting programs are available upon request.

Hide and Seek Foundation
P.O. Box 722
Cornelius, OR 97113
(503) 294-0746

Services: Prevention/Education; Family Services; Parental Abduction; Abduction by Unknown Individual; Runaways; Legislative Advocate

Comment: The foundation coordinates search efforts in individual cases and offers crisis counseling and advice on a twenty-four-hour helpline. Staff members teach proper and legal methods of searching for missing children. All search coordinating is done by this national office through the Missing Children Network (see p. 138). The foundation has affiliated chapters across the country.

Oregon Child Custody Protection Association
3555 Northeast Dunlap Avenue
Albany, OR 97321
(503) 928-3448

Services: Prevention/Education; Family Services; Poster/Picture; Parental Abduction

S.C.A.R.
Springfield Child Abuse Resources
233-C North A Street
Springfield, OR 97477
(503) 746-3376

Services: Prevention/Education

Pennsylvania

Children's Rights of PA, Inc.
P.O. Box 4362
Allentown, PA 18105
(215) 437-2971
    and
P.O. Box 270
Dalton, PA 18414
(717) 563-2628

Services: Prevention/Education; Family Services; Poster/Picture; Identification Kits; Parental Abduction; Abduction by Unknown Individual; Runaways

Comment: The program operates a twenty-four-hour telephone service, works with the media to have children's pictures shown on television and to have pictures and stories printed in newspapers, and makes referrals to other agencies throughout the country.

Parents Against Child Snatching, Inc.
P.O. Box 581
Corapolis, PA 15108
(412) 264-9025

Services: Prevention/Education; Family Services; Poster/Picture; Identification Kits; Parental Abduction; Abduction by Unknown Individual; Runaways

Rhode Island

Society for Young Victims
29 Thurston Avenue
Newport, RI 02840
(401) 847-5083

Services: Prevention/Education; Family Services; Poster/Picture; Identification Kits; Parental Abduction; Abduction by Unknown Individual; Runaways

Comment: Families of runaways are also assisted through a network of citizens' band and ham radio operators who broadcast descriptions of runaways.

South Carolina

Koncepts II
P.O. Box 1962
Myrtle Beach, SC 29577
(803) 448-3097
Services: Prevention/Education

Tennessee

P.R.O.T.E.C.T.
3438 Sophia Road
Memphis, TN 38118
(901) 362-7391

Services: Prevention/Education; Family Services; Identification Kits; Legislative Advocate; Sexual Exploitation Counseling

Appendix

Tennessee Commission on Missing and Exploited Children
P.O. Box 310
Memphis, TN 38101
(901) 528-2005

Services: Prevention/Education; Identification Kits

Texas

All for the Children Foundation
P.O. Box 300505
Arlington, TX 76010
(817) 265-6430

Services: Prevention/Education; Family Services; Parental Abduction

Foundation for Missing Children
12174 Unit C
Burnet Road
Austin, TX 75758
(512) 832-1811

Services: Prevention/Education; Family Services; Poster/Picture; Identification Kits; Parental Abduction; Abduction by Unknown Individual; Runaways

Missing Children, Inc.
901 Leopard Street
P.O. Box 1958
Corpus Christi, TX 78403
(512) 888-0234
(512) 888-0236

Services: Prevention/Education; Poster/Picture; Identification Kits; Parental Abduction; Abduction by Unknown Individual; Runaways

Comment: This program is part of the police department.

Appendix

Parents of Murdered Children
Houston Chapter
8227 Roebourne Lane
Houston, TX 77070
(713) 469-0678

Services: Family Services; Legislative Advocate

Texas Child Search
P.O. Box 8122
San Antonio, TX 78208
(512) 224-7939

Services: Prevention/Education; Family Services; Poster/Picture; Parental Abduction; Abduction by Unknown Individual; Runaways

Utah

Child Find of Utah, Inc.
5755 Hansen Circle
Murray, UT 84107
(801) 261-4134
(801) 262-8056

Services: Prevention/Education; Family Services; Poster/Picture; Parental Abduction; Abduction by Unknown Individual; Runaways; Family Victim Fund

S.L.A.M.
Society's League Against Molestation
360 East 4500 South
Salt Lake City, UT 84107
(801) 328-5878

Services: Prevention/Education; Court Monitoring

Comment: The program has affiliated chapters across the country.

Vermont

Childseekers
P.O. Box 6065
Rutland, VT 05701-6065
(802) 773-5988

Services: Prevention/Education; Family Services; Newsletter

Comment: The program provides a forty-eight-hour nationwide bulletin for lost children.

TLC in VT, Inc.
P.O. Box 84
Orwelle, VT 05760
(802) 948-2115

Services: Prevention/Education; Family Services; Poster/Picture; Identification Kits; Parental Abduction; Abduction by Unknown Individual; Runaways

Virginia

Child Watch of Virginia
P.O. Box 2381
Richmond, VA 23218
(804) 346-0191

Services: Prevention/Education; Family Services; Poster/Picture; Identification Kits; Parental Abduction; Abduction by Unknown Individual; Runaways

Comment: Two neighborhood programs developed by Child Watch include a telephone alert system and a Safe Home Program. A retail merchant emergency alert system to prepare security guards and store personnel to react quickly and efficiently in the event that a child is reported missing has also been developed.

Parents Against Molesters, Inc.
P.O. Box 3557
Portsmouth, VA 23701
(804) 465-1582

Services: Prevention/Education; Family Services; Legislative Advocate

Washington

Family and Friends of Missing Persons and Violent Crime Victims
Jane Adams Building
11051 34th Street, N.E.
Seattle, WA 98125
(206) 362-1081

Services: Prevention/Education; Family Services; Poster/Picture; Parental Abduction; Abduction by Unknown Individual; Runaways; Legislative Advocate

Comment: This agency submits pictures of missing children and adults to the national media, provides grief counseling to parents and siblings, counsels families of children who have been sexually exploited, provides twenty-four-hour availability nationally, and has an adult missing persons group.

Washington Parents Coalition
11707 132nd Avenue East
Puyallup, WA 98374
(206) 848-6092

Services: Legislative Advocate

Appendix

Wisconsin

Friends of Missing Children
P.O. Box 8848
Madison, WI 53708
(608) 837-0600

Services: Parental Abduction; Abduction by Unknown Individual;
Runaways

Comment: Friends of Missing Children is composed of police officers and attorneys, working in their off-duty hours, dedicated to helping parents search for their missing children where no active police investigation exists. The staff identifies, lists, and makes available to police investigators the names of law enforcement specialists in particular types of missing or exploited children cases, assists with the coordination of search activities involving multi-jurisdictions, and provides guidelines and instructional materials to reduce liability and workload while increasing effectiveness.

Wyoming

Wyoming P.T.A.
Child Find—Missing and Abused Children
665 North 9th Street
Laramie, WY 82070
(307) 742-4504

Services: Prevention/Education; Family Services

Appendix

Canada

Canadian Centre for Missing Children
1-A Sir Winston Churchill Square
Edmonton, Alberta
Canada T5J 0R2
(403) 422-4698

Services: Poster/Picture

Child Find, British Columbia
P.O. Box 34008, Station D
Vancouver, British Columbia
Canada V6J 4W8
(604) 731-4331

Services: Prevention/Education; Family Services

Child Find, Ontario
345 Lakeshore Road, East
Suite 314
Ontario 667175
(416) 842-3535

Services: Prevention/Education

The Tania Murrell Missing Children Center
9913 151st Street
Edmonton, Alberta
Canada T5P 1T2
(403) 481-5073

Services: Family Services

Windsor Missing Children
P.O. Box 3243
Windsor, Ontario
Canada N8W 2M4
(519) 735-2712

Services: Parental Abduction

Comments: Parents are directed, when appropriate, to reasonably priced private detectives. The program has access to a lawyer, a private detective, and police officials who have donated their time and services.

ABOUT THE MAKING OF THIS BOOK

The text of *Children At Risk* was set in Bembo by Unicorn Graphics, Inc., of Washington, D.C. The book was printed and bound by Fairfield Graphics of Fairfield, Pennsylvania. The typography and binding were designed by Tom Suzuki of Falls Church, Virginia.